Cooking Pasta
with Love

Always With Love
Cooking With Love

www.thelovechef.com

OTHER BOOKS BY FRANCIS ANTHONY

Cooking with Love Italian Style

Cooking with Love: The Love Chef Shows You How

Cooking Pasta with Love

More Than 200 Delicious Recipes from the Love Chef

Francis Anthony

WILLIAM MORROW AND COMPANY, INC.

NEW YORK

It is the policy of William Morrow and Company, Inc., and its imprints and affiliates, recognizing the importance of preserving what has been written, to print the books we publish on acid-free paper, and we exert our best efforts to that end.

Library of Congress Cataloging-in-Publication Data

Anthony, Francis.
    Cooking pasta with love : more than 200 delicious recipes from the love chef / Francis Anthony.—1st ed.
        p.   cm.
    Includes index.
    ISBN 0-688-14969-3
    1. Cookery (Pasta)   I. Title.
TX809.M17A58   1998
641.8'22—dc21   97-48319
                                                            CIP

Printed in the United States of America

First Edition

1 2 3 4 5 6 7 8 9 10

BOOK DESIGN BY LISA STOKES

www.williammorrow.com

Dedicated to—
Sonnie D.
Christopher John
John Daniel
Marina Angela
Theresa F.
Christopher A.

Acknowledgments

I wish to thank the Actors Fund of America for its help with our recipe testing at its Aurora House, New York City, facility. And thanks to the many residents of Aurora House who tasted all phases of our recipe testing for their sincere and helpful input.

The Actors Fund of America is a nonprofit hardworking organization whose mission is: "To advance, foster, and benefit the welfare of all professionals in the entertainment community who are in need of help, ensuring that these efforts are accomplished with compassion, confidentiality, and preservation of dignity for the individuals concerned."

Contributions can be directed to 1501 Broadway, Suite 518, New York, N.Y. 10036.

Contents

Introduction

When I talk pasta I'm talking love . . . love of body . . . love of mind . . . love of soul. I'm talking passion . . . I'm talking foreplay—but I'm talking marriage—I'm talking Commitment—I'm talking the fusion of body, flavors, and Contentment.

The ultimate relationship . . . reaching and wanting to be perfect. And all the rest depends on you! That's why we're here *and* that's where we're going!!

Every time I prepare a recipe using pasta (either on *Live with Regis & Kathie Lee* or on other TV shows), the recipe requests are fantastic.

It's no great secret that pasta is one of America's favorite foods. Last year alone, Americans bought over 1.3 billion pounds. If it were all one-pound packages of spaghetti, those packages stacked end to end would stretch 212,595 miles or circle the earth nine times. Imagine if you calculated the distance when using each strand!

Pasta has come a long way—noodle-like food was made by the Chinese as early as 3000 B.C. Later, legend has it that Marco Polo introduced pasta to Italy following his Far East travels.

The New World first saw pasta brought by the Colonists from England. But let's give thanks to Thomas Jefferson, who is credited with bringing the first "macaroni" machine to America in 1789 from France.

And hail to the first industrial pasta factory in America, built in Brooklyn, New York (also birthplace of your love chef!).

So by popular request, here are over two hundred pasta recipes, not just Italian ones, but combinations of everyday foods married to the correct-shaped pasta. These are recipes that are simply prepared and easy to follow.

WHAT IS PASTA?

Pasta is basically a paste of flour and water, the best pasta being made with one hundred percent semolina flour from durum wheat, the hardest wheat grown.

There are so many pasta shapes and sizes that for a long time certain manufacturers put numbers on their packages to make a specific cut more easily identifiable. Many a time Mom sent me to the store and gave me a piece of paper with a number on it for the pasta I had to buy.

Today I notice that many supermarkets stock only the more popular cuts, such as spaghetti, linguine, ziti, rotelle, and penne. However, do look for and sample other cuts, like shells. If you were to cook various pastas with a different sauce every night, it would be years before you'd run out of recipes.

Spaghetti, linguine, and fettuccine are great for sauces that cling, while shaped pastas such as ziti, penne, and shells are ideal with vegetables and beans. And the tiniest shapes— ditalini, acini di pepe, and pastina—are wonderful additions to soups, stews, and chowders. Although they are all made with flour and water, each shape adds it own unique character to a particular sauce or topping.

PASTA NUTRITION

Pasta delivers a bona fide nutritional boost that is rich in complex carbohydrates, which is basically Mother Nature's "time release" of energy. The carbohydrates become glucose stored in the muscles, and are released as needed by the body. This is why athletes chow down on pasta before an event.

In fact, the USDA's food guide pyramid recommends we eat six to eleven servings of complex carbohydrates daily. A typical serving size is two ounces of dried pasta, which is 210 calories.

Pasta contains no cholesterol and is usually enriched with iron and B vitamins. In a world with labels this could be truly called a "health food."

In keeping pace with healthful recipes, I've used ingredients that reduce the fat content of the overall recipe while still maintaining its taste.

The pairing of vegetables, utilizing flavorful sautéing, creates a sauce of its own.

COOKING PASTA

Dried pasta, the type you find on supermarket shelves, is easy to store and easy to cook correctly. For each pound of pasta, start with 6 quarts of fresh cold water in a large covered pot. The water must be boiling before you add the pasta. I do not add the traditional 2 tablespoons of salt to the boiling water. But try it both ways and you be the judge. You should add the pasta gradually to the boiling water in order to maintain the water temperature. Cover the pot until the water comes to a boil again, then remove the cover and add 1 teaspoon of olive oil. This will keep the pasta from sticking.

Stir frequently, cooking until the pasta is firm yet tender—al dente, which literally translates as "to the tooth." And that's what you must do—bite a piece during cooking to test the firmness. Remember, each shape has a different length of cooking time. Fresh pasta, as opposed to dried pasta, cooks much more quickly, but remember that most fresh pasta also contains eggs. When pasta is cooked, you must be ready to serve it almost immediately.

When measuring the quantity of dried pasta for cooking, a good rule of thumb is using two ounces of raw pasta for an appetizer portion and three to four ounces for a main course. This is the reason most of the recipes serve four to six. And finally, remember that dried pasta expands when cooked, while fresh pasta does not.

Tips to Enhance Your Pasta Enjoyment

When you prepare my recipes, please realize that using extra condiments, such as grated cheese and crushed red pepper, and garnishes such as parsley and fresh herbs, are up to your individual taste.

While we're on the subject of cheese, I would recommend you buy a wedge of Parmesan, Romano, and other grating cheeses in the cheese department of a supermarket and have them grate it for you. You'll be surprised at the taste difference from those supermarket-shaker varieties. The freshly grated cheeses are also more economical.

A SECRET . . .

I know it's difficult to fit all the pasta in a skillet for final saucing, but by heating them together, it lets the flavor permeate the pasta much better.

Pasta with Vegetables

Mother Nature's vast palette from the earth gives us the nourishing partner for many contrasting textures and flavors to tease, satisfy, and cajole every taste.

Here, the various sizes and shapes of pasta can be matched with what your garden, green market, season, and budget dictate.

You'll find some odd yet delicious combinations—my full-bodied pasta I call "Hot and Spicy Puerto Rican Pasta" is a sauce made with capers, olives, peppers, onions, and perfumed cilantro. And when your family tastes my pasta shells with red potatoes, they'll be on time for dinner every night.

Mediterranean Pasta

The countries that surround the Mediterranean enjoy olive oil, olives, rich spices, and feta cheese. Mixed with small shells, this dish captures all the flavor.

1 pound small shells
1 clove garlic
2 tablespoons extra-virgin olive oil
2 medium potatoes, diced
2 medium carrots, diced
1 small red onion, chopped
2 medium zucchini, diced
6 ripe plum tomatoes, diced
½ teaspoon ground cumin
¼ teaspoon ground turmeric
Salt to taste (optional)
¼ teaspoon ground white pepper
1 teaspoon hot sauce
4 ounces crumbled feta cheese
½ cup pitted black olives, sliced
¼ cup chopped parsley, for garnish

SERVES 4 TO 6

~

Cook the pasta (see page xiii).

In a large skillet, sauté the garlic in the olive oil and discard when it turns brown. Add the potatoes and carrots, and when almost soft, add the onion, zucchini, and tomatoes. Add the cumin, turmeric, salt, pepper, and hot sauce. Combine the mixture with the pasta and toss the cheese and olives on top. Garnish with the parsley and serve.

✎ Hungarian Noodles

Many years ago, one of my cooking school instructors created a Hungarian menu for her class. The intense flavor of the many dishes led me to construct this tasty dish.

1 large onion, chopped
3 tablespoons extra-virgin olive oil
2 tablespoons unsalted butter
1 medium green cabbage, cored and shredded
½ cup chicken stock
1 teaspoon brown sugar
2½ teaspoons sweet paprika
Juice of ½ lemon
Salt to taste
1 pound wide noodles
2 tablespoons poppy seeds
2 cups nonfat sour cream

SERVES 4 TO 6

In a large skillet, sauté the onion in the oil and butter until translucent. Add the cabbage, chicken stock, sugar, paprika, lemon juice, and salt. Continue to sauté until the cabbage is lightly browned.

Meanwhile, cook the noodles (see page xiii). When the noodles and cabbage are ready, toss together with the poppy seeds and sour cream and serve.

Middle Eastern Pasta

I enjoy an eggplant many ways. Here, with a scent of spice and mixed with sour cream, it takes on an independent superiority.

1 large eggplant, peeled and halved
1 pound medium shells
1 clove garlic, minced
¼ cup extra-virgin olive oil
½ teaspoon ground turmeric
1 tablespoon ground cumin
Juice of ½ lemon
Freshly ground black pepper to taste
1 cup sour cream
Salt to taste (optional)

SERVES 4 TO 6

To cook the eggplant:

Oven method:
Preheat the oven to 350°F. Bake the eggplant until soft, about 1 hour and 15 minutes.

Microwave method:
To microwave the eggplant, cut into ¼-inch cubes and place in a microwaveable dish on high power for 6 to 8 minutes, or until soft.

Meanwhile, cook the pasta (see page xiii).

Mash the cooked eggplant and set aside. Meanwhile, sauté the garlic in olive oil until it turns golden. Add the mashed eggplant and sauté, stirring continuously. Add the turmeric, cumin, lemon juice, pepper, and sour cream, adding salt, if desired. Mix with the pasta and serve.

Ziti with Eggplant

8 cloves garlic, thinly sliced
1 small onion, chopped
2 red bell peppers, cut into thin strips
½ cup extra-virgin olive oil
1 medium eggplant, peeled and chopped
1 tablespoon dried oregano
½ teaspoon crushed red pepper
Juice of ½ lemon
1 pound ziti
12 green olives, pitted and sliced
1 tablespoon capers, rinsed
2 tablespoons chopped Italian parsley
½ cup pasta water
Freshly ground black pepper to taste
Salt to taste (optional)
Grated Parmesan cheese as garnish

SERVES 4 TO 6

In a large skillet, sauté the garlic, onion, and red peppers in olive oil until soft. Add the eggplant, oregano, red pepper, and lemon juice. Cover and cook for about 20 minutes.

Meanwhile, cook the pasta (see page xiii). Reserve ½ cup water when draining.

To the mixture, add the olives, capers, and parsley and cook for another 10 minutes. Mix in the water, pepper, and salt. Toss with the pasta, sprinkle with the cheese, and serve.

Orzo with Cabbage

The perfect appetizer or side dish to accompany a pork roast or leg of lamb.

8 ounces orzo
½ cup golden raisins
½ cup cider vinegar
1 medium cabbage, cored and shredded
½ teaspoon ground turmeric
2 tablespoons pine nuts
1 tablespoon brown sugar
Salt to taste (optional)
Freshly ground black pepper to taste

SERVES 4 TO 6

Cook the pasta (see page xiii).

Preheat the oven to 350°F.

Grease a large baking dish. In a small bowl, soak the raisins in the vinegar. When the raisins are plump, drain, reserving the vinegar. Place half of the cabbage in the baking dish.

In a medium bowl, mix the orzo, turmeric, pine nuts, raisins, brown sugar, salt, and pepper together. Spread the mixture over the cabbage, and cover with the remaining cabbage. Drizzle the top with the reserved vinegar. Bake at 350°F uncovered, for 35 to 45 minutes, and serve.

Angel Hair with Almonds alla Liz

1 cup sliced almonds
1 tablespoon unsalted butter
2 tablespoons extra-virgin olive oil
1 bunch scallions or green onions, sliced
½ cup light cream
3 tablespoons creamy peanut butter
¼ teaspoon white pepper
Salt to taste (optional)
½ pound angel hair

SERVES 4

In a large skillet, lightly brown the almonds in butter, remove and set aside. Add the olive oil and scallions, sauté briefly and add cream. Blend in the peanut butter, and add the pepper and salt and simmer until the mixture is thickened.

Meanwhile, cook the pasta (see page xiii).

Add the browned almonds to the sauce. When the pasta is cooked, drain, toss with sauce, and serve.

Pasta with Sun-dried Tomatoes

1 pound penne
3 cloves garlic
6 plum tomatoes, chopped
¼ cup extra-virgin olive oil
¾ cup sun-dried tomatoes, marinated in olive oil, drained and diced
½ teaspoon dried basil
Salt to taste (optional)
Freshly ground black pepper to taste
Shavings of Romano cheese for garnish

SERVES 4 TO 6

Cook the pasta (see page xiii).

Sauté the garlic and plum tomatoes in olive oil until soft. Add the sun-dried tomatoes, basil, salt and pepper. Toss with pasta, garnish with cheese, and serve.

Pasta alla Puttanesca

The original recipe for this spicy sauce is said to have originated with some naughty ladies of ancient Naples. Here's my "good guy" version.

2 cloves garlic
4 tablespoons extra-virgin olive oil
2 anchovy fillets
One 35-ounce can Italian plum tomatoes, undrained and coarsely
   chopped
1 dozen pitted black olives, chopped
1 small pimento, chopped
2 sprigs basil
1 tablespoon capers
¼ teaspoon crushed red pepper
Freshly ground black pepper to taste
1 tablespoon finely chopped fresh parsley
1 pound linguine

SERVES 4 TO 6

Sauté the garlic in the oil, and add the anchovies. When the anchovies start to fall apart in the oil, add the tomatoes with their juice. Then add the olives, pimento, basil, and capers. Continue stirring and add the crushed red pepper, black pepper, and parsley. Cook for no longer than 18 minutes. Cook the linguine until al dente and serve the sauce over the pasta.

Pasta with White Beans

2 cloves garlic
1 medium onion, chopped
2 plum tomatoes, chopped
1 medium carrot, chopped
2 tablespoons extra-virgin olive oil
1 cup beef stock
One 19-ounce can Great Northern beans, undrained
¼ teaspoon ground nutmeg
Salt to taste (optional)
¼ teaspoon white pepper
8 ounces plain low-fat yogurt
¼ cup grated Parmesan cheese
1 pound shells

SERVES 4 TO 6

In a medium skillet, sauté the garlic, onion, tomatoes, and carrot in the olive oil. Discard the garlic when it turns golden. When the onions are translucent, add the beef stock, beans, nutmeg, salt, and pepper. Cover and simmer for 20 minutes.

Remove the cover, add the yogurt and cheese, and simmer for another 15 minutes.

Meanwhile, cook the pasta (see page xiii). Toss with the bean mixture and serve.

⫸ Pasta with Black Beans

1 cup dried black beans
1 medium onion, chopped
3 cloves garlic
¼ cup extra-virgin olive oil
1 can beef stock
1 cup tomato sauce
½ cup chopped fresh cilantro, plus several sprigs for garnish
Freshly ground black pepper to taste
Salt to taste (optional)
1 pound orecchiette
½ cup sour cream, for garnish

SERVES 4 TO 6

Place the beans in a saucepan and cover with cold water, at least a few inches above the beans. Cover and bring to a boil. Boil for 2 to 3 minutes; turn off heat, and let soak, covered, for at least one hour. Drain.

In a large skillet, sauté the onion and garlic in the olive oil until soft. Then add the beef stock, sauce, cilantro, pepper, and salt. Add fresh drained beans to mixture and continue to simmer, covered, for about 1½ hours.

Meanwhile, cook the pasta (see page xiii).

Spoon the pasta and dress with the bean sauce. Top with a dollop of sour cream and a sprig of cilantro and serve.

Kidney Beans and Pasta

1 medium onion, chopped
2 ribs celery, sliced
2 tablespoons extra-virgin olive oil
One 15- to 18-ounce can kidney beans, undrained
2 tablespoons tomato paste
½ cup chicken stock
1 teaspoon brown sugar
½ teaspoon white pepper
1 teaspoon dried oregano
1 tablespoon fresh lemon juice
Salt to taste (optional)
1 pound medium shells

SERVES 4 TO 6

In a large skillet, sauté the onion and celery in the olive oil until the onion is translucent. Add the beans and stir in the tomato paste and stock. Add the brown sugar, pepper, oregano, lemon juice, and salt and simmer for 15 minutes.

Meanwhile, cook the pasta (see page xiii). When the pasta is ready, combine with the bean mixture and serve.

Pasta with Red Bell Pepper Sauce

A fully ripened pepper turns red and its taste is far superior to that of a green pepper. Also, it contains more vitamin C than an orange.

4 medium red bell peppers
1 small onion
1 cup chicken stock
2 cloves garlic
2 tablespoons extra-virgin olive oil
1 teaspoon dried basil
½ teaspoon crushed red pepper flakes
½ cup heavy cream
½ cup Parmesan cheese
Freshly ground black pepper to taste
Salt to taste (optional)
1 pound penne

SERVES 4 TO 6

Purée the peppers, onion, and chicken stock in a food processor.

In a large skillet, sauté the garlic in oil. Add the puréed mixture, dried basil, and crushed red pepper. Simmer and add the cream and cheese; continue to cook until slightly reduced and thick, 20 to 30 minutes. Add the pepper and salt, if desired.

Meanwhile, cook the pasta (see page xiii). Drain, toss with mixture, and serve.

Pasta with Kohlrabi

Indigenous to Central Europe, kohlrabi has a buttery, nutty flavor, especially when sautéed. It is the perfect match for pasta.

8 bulbs kohlrabi
2 cloves garlic, minced
3 tablespoons extra-virgin olive oil
1 teaspoon balsamic vinegar
1 tablespoon fresh lemon juice
2 cups chicken stock
Salt to taste (optional)
Freshly ground black pepper to taste
1 pound rigatoni
½ cup grated Romano cheese
Crushed red pepper (optional)

SERVES 4 TO 6

Clean the kohlrabi, peel the bulbs, and slice in half. Tops can be discarded unless they are young and tender. (Save for future use.)

In a large skillet, sauté the kohlrabi slices and the garlic in the olive oil, then add the vinegar and lemon juice. Add the chicken stock, cover, and simmer for 35 to 40 minutes. Season with salt and pepper.

Meanwhile, cook the pasta (see page xiii).

In a large bowl, combine the pasta and cheese with the kohlrabi mixture. Toss well, garnish with red pepper, if desired, and serve.

Pasta with Escarole

3 cloves garlic
4 tablespoons extra-virgin olive oil
1 slice baked ham, 1/4 inch thick, chopped
1 can anchovy fillets, drained and rinsed
1/2 cup green olives stuffed with pimento, sliced
1 cup chicken stock
1 1/2 to 2 pounds escarole, chopped
1/4 teaspoon dried thyme
Freshly ground black pepper to taste
Salt to taste (optional)
1/4 teaspoon crushed red pepper
1 pound rigatoni
1 cup pasta water
1/2 cup Parmesan cheese

SERVES 4 TO 6

In a large skillet, sauté the garlic in olive oil. Discard the garlic when golden. Add the ham, anchovies, and green olives, and sauté until the anchovies are blended into the oil. Add the chicken broth, escarole, thyme, pepper, salt, and crushed red pepper. Cover.

Meanwhile, cook the pasta (see page xiii). Reserve 1 cup water when draining.

Cook the escarole until tender, adding pasta water if necessary. When it is ready, add the cheese. Toss with the pasta and serve.

❧ Pasta-stuffed Tomatoes

*Bring them to your next potluck dinner and you will be the "king or queen."
Just make sure you have one for every guest.*

8 ounces spinach noodles
6 large, ripe tomatoes
½ teaspoon dried thyme
½ cup grated Parmesan cheese
4 ounces blue cheese
2 tablespoons extra-virgin olive oil
⅛ teaspoon white pepper

SERVES 4 TO 6

❧

Preheat the oven to 350°F.

Cook the pasta (see page xiii).

Cut the tops off the tomatoes, slice off the bottoms, and scoop out the insides. Season the insides with ¼ teaspoon thyme and sprinkle with ¼ cup of the grated cheese. Place in an oiled baking dish and bake for 12 to 15 minutes.

Meanwhile, in a large skillet, melt the blue cheese in olive oil, add the pepper, the balance of thyme, and the balance of the grated cheese. Add the noodles to the skillet and quickly stir in the cheese sauce.

Fill the tomatoes with the noodles and bake for an additional 6 minutes. Leftover noodles can be used as a bed under the tomatoes when serving.

Pasta with Mushrooms and Hazelnuts

Today's exotic mushrooms are available in most supermarkets. When combined with toasted hazelnuts, they yield a robust, intense flavor.

8 ounces exotic mushroom mixture (such as shiitake, oyster, or
   chanterelle), chopped
½ cup sherry
1 pound tagliatelle
2 tablespoons unsalted butter
2 tablespoons all-purpose flour
1 cup heavy cream
½ cup whole milk
3 shallots, minced
Freshly ground nutmeg to taste
Salt to taste (optional)
¼ teaspoon white pepper
¼ cup toasted hazelnuts, ground (see box)
½ cup grated Romano cheese

SERVES 4 TO 6

Soak the mushrooms in the sherry for at least 30 minutes.

Meanwhile, cook the pasta (see page xiii).

In a medium saucepan, melt the butter, add the flour, and sauté into a tan roux. Meanwhile, whisk in the cream and milk. Add the shallots, nutmeg, salt, and pepper. Add the hazelnuts, cheese, and mushrooms with the sherry. Simmer until thick, about 30 minutes.

In a large bowl, combine the pasta and sauce, toss well, and serve.

> To toast the hazelnuts, shell and place them on an ungreased baking sheet and toast in the oven at 300°F for 20 minutes.

Greek Pasta Salad

This is a great dish for buffet or picnic—the perfect warm-weather dish!

When I created this recipe for a national tour, I watched people lining up for a taste, commenting, "This is the best ever!"

1 pound tricolor pasta
4 plum tomatoes, diced
12 pitted black olives, sliced
1 medium red onion, chopped
½ teaspoon dried basil
½ teaspoon dried thyme
2 cloves garlic, blanched and minced
4 tablespoons extra-virgin olive oil
4 tablespoons balsamic vinegar
1 tablespoon fresh lemon juice
4 ounces feta cheese, crumbled (optional, more if desired)
Salt to taste (optional)
Freshly ground black pepper to taste

SERVES 8 TO 10

Cook the pasta (see page xiii), drain well, and immediately rinse in cold water. Shake off the excess water and chill.

In a large mixing bowl, add the tomatoes, olives, onion, basil, thyme, garlic, olive oil, vinegar, lemon juice, and chilled pasta, and then top with the cheese. Toss well, adding salt and pepper. Refrigerate for at least 2 hours before serving.

◦ Chickpea and Olive Pasta Salad

A perfect dish for a picnic. Accompany with some rosemary-roasted chicken, Pinot Grigio wine and a loaf of semolina bread—a delicious combination.

1 pound ditali
One 16-ounce can chickpeas, undrained
2 cloves garlic, blanched and minced
One 6-ounce can pitted black olives, sliced
1 small red onion, chopped
¼ cup extra-virgin olive oil
Juice of ½ lime
2 tablespoons fresh cilantro, chopped
Freshly ground black pepper to taste
Salt to taste (optional)

SERVES 4 TO 6

Cook the pasta (see page xiii). Rinse, drain well, and immediately rinse in cold water. Shake off the excess water and chill.

In a medium bowl, combine the pasta with the chickpeas, garlic, olives, onions, oil, lime juice, cilantro, pepper, and salt. Toss well and serve.

~ Shells with Red Potatoes

In a certain region of Italy, pasta with potatoes is a distinctive dish. This recipe will satisfy your family without the trip to Italy.

1 pound medium shells
1 pound red potatoes, diced
4 tablespoons extra-virgin olive oil
1 large onion, diced
One 16-ounce can plum tomatoes, chopped
1 teaspoon dried basil
¼ teaspoon dried thyme
¼ teaspoon crushed red pepper
Salt to taste (optional)
Freshly ground black pepper to taste
¼ cup grated Parmesan cheese

SERVES 4 TO 6

Cook the pasta (see page xiii).

Sauté the potatoes in the olive oil in a large skillet. When the potatoes are almost cooked, add the onion, and cook until the onion is translucent. Add the tomatoes with juice, basil, thyme, crushed red pepper, salt, and pepper. Cover and simmer for 15 to 18 minutes.

Add the cooked pasta to the sauce, toss with the cheese, and serve.

Pasta with Cauliflower

1 head fresh cauliflower, cut into bite-size pieces (or two 10-ounce
    packages frozen cauliflower florets)
3 cloves garlic, crushed
1 tablespoon unsalted butter
2 tablespoons extra-virgin olive oil
½ cup white wine
1 pound rigatoni
½ cup pasta water
3 tablespoons grated Parmesan cheese
½ cup fresh Italian parsley, chopped
Salt to taste (optional)
Freshly ground black pepper to taste

SERVES 4 TO 6

Steam the cauliflower in the pasta pot until almost cooked.
Meanwhile, in a large skillet, sauté the garlic in the butter and oil and discard the garlic when golden. Add the cauliflower to the skillet and sauté
until lightly brown, and add the wine.

Meanwhile, cook the pasta (see page xiii). Reserve ½ cup of the pasta
water when draining. Add water and the cauliflower mixture; toss with the
pasta. Sprinkle with Parmesan cheese, parsley, and season with salt and
pepper. Serve.

Summer Pasta with Peas

1 pound radiators
1 tablespoon unsalted butter
2 tablespoons extra-virgin olive oil
1 clove garlic, minced
1 small onion, chopped
1 1/2 cups chicken stock
1/2 teaspoon dried summer savory
One 10-ounce package frozen peas
Grated Parmesan cheese to sprinkle on top
Salt to taste (optional)
Freshly ground black pepper to taste
Crushed red pepper (optional)

SERVES 4 TO 6

Cook the pasta (see page xiii).

In a large skillet, heat the butter and the oil, and add the garlic and onion. When the onions are translucent, add the chicken stock and reduce the heat slightly, and cook for 3 or 4 minutes. Add the summer savory and peas. Add the pasta and toss with the mixture. Add the Parmesan cheese, salt, and pepper, and red pepper, if desired, and serve.

Substitute 10 ounces lima beans for the peas.

Pasta with Peppers

I remember one year when my parents' garden produced a bumper crop of peppers and I used them all up with this wonderful pasta.

1 pound ziti or penne
1 tablespoon unsalted butter
2 tablespoons extra-virgin olive oil
1½ pounds red and green peppers, cut into strips
2 cloves garlic
1 medium onion, chopped
1 cup chicken stock
¼ teaspoon dried oregano
¼ cup grated Parmesan cheese
Salt to taste (optional)
Freshly ground black pepper to taste
Crushed red pepper (optional)

SERVES 4 TO 6

Cook the pasta (see page xiii).

In a large skillet, heat the butter and add the oil. Add the peppers, garlic, and onion and sauté until the garlic is golden; discard. Continue to cook until the onions are translucent and the peppers are soft. Add the chicken stock and reduce the heat slightly, and cook for 8 to 10 minutes. Add the oregano. Add the pasta and toss with the mixture. Add the Parmesan cheese, salt, and pepper, and red pepper, if desired, and serve.

Pasta with Artichokes

We all enjoy stuffed artichokes, but the nutty flavor and tenderness of baby artichokes makes them an ideal candidate for a liaison with pasta.

½ cup extra-virgin olive oil
8 small (baby) artichokes, trimmed, choke removed, and cut into thin
   wedges
1 large red bell pepper, seeded and cut into thin strips
1 medium onion, chopped
3 cloves garlic
½ cup chicken stock
½ cup dry white wine
Juice of ½ lemon
¼ teaspoon crushed red pepper
¼ cup heavy cream
1 pound fettucine or linguine
¼ cup grated Parmesan cheese
Freshly ground black pepper to taste
Salt to taste (optional)

SERVES 4 TO 6

Heat the olive oil over medium heat in a large skillet. Add the artichokes, red pepper strips, onion, and garlic and cook 2 to 3 minutes, stirring frequently. Discard the garlic when it turns golden. Add the chicken stock, wine, lemon juice, and crushed red pepper. Reduce the heat to low, cover, and cook until the artichoke pieces are soft, about 15 minutes. Add cream and cook for another 5 to 10 minutes.

Meanwhile, cook the pasta (see page xiii).

Toss the pasta with the artichoke mixture, add the cheese, pepper, and salt and serve.

Spaghetti Oregano

The ingredients in this dish are deceptively simple, yet the taste is quite delicious.

1 cup bread crumbs
½ cup extra-virgin olive oil
24 large or jumbo pitted black olives, chopped
4 cloves garlic
¾ cup dry white wine
1 tablespoon dried oregano
1 pound spaghetti
¾ cup grated Parmesan cheese
Freshly ground black pepper to taste
Salt to taste (optional)
½ cup chopped Italian parsley

SERVES 4 TO 6

Toast the bread crumbs in a large skillet until lightly brown. Remove and set aside.

Heat the olive oil over medium heat. Add the olives and garlic and cook for 1 minute, stirring frequently. Discard the garlic when it turns golden. Add the wine and oregano, and cook for about 4 minutes.

Meanwhile, cook the pasta (see page xiii).

Return the pasta to the saucepan, and stir in the toasted bread crumbs, cheese, pepper, and salt. Sprinkle with parsley and serve.

LINGUINE AND ANCHOVY OIL

Follow the recipe but replace the spaghetti with linguine and add 6 anchovy fillets, or a 2-ounce can, to the hot oil at the last minute and blend in. Add 1 teaspoon of crushed red pepper.

Linguine with Scallions and Bread Crumbs

In the confines of a friend's galley aboard his yacht, I prepared this simple yet tasty pasta that was the hit of our sailing day.

1 pound linguine
1 cup extra-virgin olive oil
2 cloves garlic
1 bunch scallions, thinly sliced
12 green olives, chopped
2½ cups plain bread crumbs
Crushed red pepper (optional)
Salt to taste (optional)
½ cup chopped Italian parsley
Freshly ground black pepper to taste

SERVES 4 AS A MAIN COURSE OR 6 TO 8 AS AN APPETIZER

Cook the pasta (see page xiii).

Meanwhile, heat ½ cup of the oil in a medium skillet, sauté the garlic until golden, and discard it. Add the scallions and sauté until translucent.

In another skillet, heat the remaining oil and add the olives and bread crumbs. Cook until the bread crumbs are golden, about 10 minutes.

Drain the pasta and immediately toss with the scallions, crushed red pepper, and salt. Top individual servings of the pasta with the bread crumb mixture. Sprinkle with parsley and black pepper. Serve immediately.

Pasta with Broccoli

The hallmark of Italian cooking is elegant simplicity, and this intensely flavorful dish is a great example of why this Mediterranean cuisine is so popular. Try making the dish with extra-virgin olive oil—you'll taste the difference.

1 bunch broccoli
½ cup extra-virgin olive oil
1 large red bell pepper, seeded and cut into thin strips
2 cloves garlic, peeled
½ cup water
½ cup dry white wine
1 pound fettuccine or linguine
¼ cup unsalted butter
¼ cup grated Parmesan cheese
Freshly ground black pepper to taste
Salt to taste (optional)

SERVES 4 TO 6

Trim the leaves and tough ends from each stalk of broccoli and peel off the skin. Cut the stalks into 1-inch-long pieces and the head into small florets.

In a large skillet, heat the olive oil over medium heat. Add the broccoli, red pepper strips, and garlic and cook for 1 minute, stirring frequently. Discard the garlic when it turns golden. Add the water and wine, reduce the heat to low, cover, and cook until the broccoli is just tender, but firm, about 5 minutes.

Meanwhile, cook the pasta (see page xiii). Drain, return the pasta to the saucepan, and toss with the butter. Stir in the broccoli mixture, cheese, pepper, and salt and serve.

Asparagus with Pasta

Asparagus was prized by the ancient Romans (including one or two in my family) for its medicinal value (significant vitamin C, good potassium, excellent folic acid, plus fiber) as well as its wonderful taste.

Choose thick or thin stalks, according to your preference. By the way, I do not peel asparagus but just cut or break off the woody, pulpy ends.

1½ pounds asparagus, cut on bias into 1½-inch pieces
1 tablespoon unsalted butter
2 tablespoons extra-virgin olive oil
1 clove garlic
1 small onion, chopped
½ cup chicken stock
1 pound ziti or penne
¼ cup grated Parmesan cheese
Salt to taste (optional)
Freshly ground black pepper to taste
Crushed red pepper (optional)

SERVES 4 TO 6

Steam the asparagus in a covered stockpot and cook until almost tender. Meanwhile, in a large skillet, heat the butter and the oil over medium heat. Add the garlic and onion. Discard the garlic when it turns golden. Add the asparagus to the skillet and sauté for 2 minutes, then add the stock and cook for another 5 minutes.

Meanwhile, cook the pasta (see page xiii) and toss with the mixture. Add the Parmesan cheese, salt, pepper, and red pepper, if desired, and serve.

❧Turnip Greens with Pasta

Two of my favorite ingredients in one dish—turnip greens and pasta. The dish has a surprisingly sweet and sour flavor from the balsamic vinegar.

2 pounds turnip greens
½ cup water
2 cloves garlic, crushed
3 tablespoons extra-virgin olive oil
½ teaspoon balsamic vinegar
1 tablespoon fresh lemon juice
Salt to taste (optional)
Freshly ground black pepper to taste
1 pound shells
Crushed red pepper (optional)

SERVES 4 TO 6

Clean the greens, cut off the bottoms, and chop into small pieces.
Steam the greens in the water in a large covered skillet.

In another large skillet, sauté the garlic in the olive oil, then add the vinegar and lemon juice. Add the greens and cover until cooked to your taste. Season with salt and pepper.

Meanwhile, cook the pasta (see page xiii) and drain. Mix with the greens, garnish with red pepper, if desired, and serve.

Spaghetti with Fresh Parsley

I bet you never thought that you could fry up a big bunch of parsley and have something terrific come of it!

1 cup bread crumbs
½ cup extra-virgin olive oil
2½ cups whole fresh Italian parsley leaves, stems removed
4 cloves garlic
Salt to taste (optional)
½ cup pasta water
½ cup dry white wine
1 pound spaghetti
¾ cup grated Parmesan cheese
Freshly ground black pepper to taste

SERVES 4 TO 6

Toast the bread crumbs in a large skillet until lightly brown. Remove and set aside.

Heat the oil in the same skillet over medium heat and add the parsley and garlic; cook for 1 minute. Remove the parsley with a slotted spoon, add the salt, and set aside. Discard the garlic when it turns golden. Add the water and wine and heat for about 2 minutes.

Meanwhile, cook the pasta (see page xiii). Drain, and return to the saucepan. Stir in the toasted bread crumbs, fried parsley, cheese, and pepper.

Substitute cilantro or basil for the parsley and cook as directed above.

Pasta and Cottage Cheese

*That leftover cottage cheese in the back of the refrigerator finally has a use.
Buy enough or more to equal 2 cups and you have a delicious and new-tasting
pasta.*

1 pound ziti
2 tablespoons unsalted butter
Freshly grated nutmeg to taste
Freshly ground black pepper to taste
½ bunch scallions, thinly sliced
2 cups low-fat creamed small curd cottage cheese

SERVES 4 TO 6

Cook the pasta (see page xiii). Mix the butter and add the nutmeg,
pepper, and scallions and stir in the cottage cheese. Serve.

South Carolina Pasta with Okra and Tomatoes

If you are buying okra, it should be fresh and on the small side. Lay the okra on a cookie sheet and place in a warm oven at 175°F for about 45 minutes. When buying frozen okra, do not let it defrost. Use it frozen.

3 tablespoons of extra-virgin olive oil
1 clove garlic
2 small onions, chopped
1 bay leaf
1 pound fresh okra, cut up, or one 10-ounce package, frozen
One 32-ounce can plum tomatoes, chopped
½ teaspoon dried thyme
½ teaspoon balsamic vinegar
Salt to taste (optional)
Freshly ground black pepper to taste
1 pound penne

SERVES 4 TO 6

In a medium skillet, heat the oil and sauté the garlic, onions, and bay leaf. Discard the garlic when it turns golden. Add the okra and sauté for 3 to 4 minutes, and add the tomatoes, thyme, vinegar, salt, and pepper. Cover and simmer for 15 to 20 minutes, or until the okra is cooked.

Meanwhile, cook the pasta (see page xiii).

Toss the pasta with the okra sauce. Discard the bay leaf and serve.

Hot and Spicy Puerto Rican Pasta

Everyone should visit this gem in the Caribbean. This dish is my tribute to the beautiful island for the many times I've dined there.

1 pound rigatoni
¼ cup extra-virgin olive oil
1 large onion, chopped
1 medium red bell pepper, seeded and chopped
1 medium green pepper, seeded and chopped
1 bunch cilantro
1 tablespoon capers
12 Spanish olives, sliced
3 cloves garlic, minced
2 tablespoons tomato paste
1 cup tomato sauce
1 cup pasta water
1 teaspoon crushed red pepper
Freshly ground black pepper to taste
Salt to taste (optional)

SERVES 4 TO 6

Cook the pasta (see page xiii). Reserve 1 cup water when draining.

In a large skillet, heat the oil over medium heat and sauté the onion, peppers, and fresh cilantro until the onion is translucent. Add the capers, olives, and garlic, and stir in the tomato paste, tomato sauce, and water. Cook, covered, for about 20 minutes.

Add the crushed red pepper, black pepper, and salt. Spoon over each serving of pasta and serve.

Noodles with Garlic and White Mushrooms

I can picture serving this pasta on a mild summer evening in a palatial setting, sipping on some white wine.

12 ounces noodles
2 tablespoons extra-virgin olive oil
2 tablespoons butter
2 cloves garlic
½ cup sliced scallions
1½ cups sliced white mushrooms
1 cup chicken stock
¾ cup dry white wine
¼ teaspoon white pepper
Salt to taste (optional)
2 tablespoons flour
½ cup milk or 2 tablespoons heavy cream
¼ cup chopped Italian parsley

SERVES 4

Cook the pasta (see page xiii).

In a large skillet, heat the oil and butter and sauté the garlic and scallions until the scallions are translucent. Add the mushrooms, stock, wine, white pepper, and salt. Combine the flour with the milk or cream and add to the skillet, stirring well. Cook until the sauce is thickened, 10 to 12 minutes. Add the parsley and serve over the noodles.

Oklahoma Whole-wheat Spaghetti

Although pasta is made from durum wheat, I have chosen whole-wheat spaghetti in honor of this wheat-producing state.

1 pound whole wheat spaghetti
1 clove garlic, minced
2 small turnips, diced
2 carrots, finely diced
3 tablespoons extra-virgin olive oil
2 ripe medium tomatoes, chopped
One 15-ounce can black beans, undrained
1 cup water
½ teaspoon dried savory
Salt to taste (optional)
Freshly ground black pepper to taste

SERVES 4 TO 6

Cook the pasta (see page xiii). Reserve 1 cup of water when draining.

In a large skillet, sauté the garlic, turnips, and carrots in the olive oil until carrots are almost soft. Add the tomatoes, black beans, water, savory, salt, and pepper. Simmer, covered, for 15 minutes. Spoon over servings of pasta and serve.

❧ New Jersey Pasta

I eat tomatoes only at the height of their season. On the East Coast, it's New Jersey tomatoes in the summer. They are filled with a sweetness not easily matched.

1 pound mafalde
3 large, very ripe tomatoes (preferably Jersey), chopped
3 tablespoons extra-virgin olive oil
1 teaspoon dried summer savory
½ cup chopped fresh basil
1 cup heavy cream
½ cup grated Romano cheese
Freshly ground black pepper to taste
Salt to taste (optional)

SERVES 4

⧲

Cook the pasta (see page xiii).

In a large skillet, sauté the tomatoes in olive oil. Add the summer savory and basil, and continue to cook for 4 to 6 minutes.

Add the cream, cheese, pepper, and salt, and simmer until the mixture is slightly thickened, 12 to 15 minutes. Toss with the pasta and serve.

New Mexico Gazpacho

This is a hearty pasta vegetable soup with a flavor reminiscent of gazpacho.

1/2 cup chicken stock
1 1/2 cups V-8 juice
5 to 6 ripe tomatoes, seeded and cored
1 cucumber, seeded
1 medium onion, grated
1 medium green bell pepper, cored, seeded, and quartered
2 sprigs fresh basil
1 clove garlic
1/4 teaspoon dried dill weed
1/4 teaspoon ground cumin
Dash of hot pepper sauce
1 tablespoon red wine vinegar
1 tablespoon fresh lemon juice
Salt to taste (optional)
Freshly ground black pepper to taste
1 cup half-and-half
1 pound spinach or tortellini

SERVES 4 TO 6

Put the stock and V-8 juice in a large saucepan. Bring to a simmer. Using the steel blade of a food processor, purée the tomatoes, cucumber, onion, pepper, basil, garlic, dill weed, cumin, hot pepper, vinegar, and lemon juice. Process in 2 batches, if necessary. Pour the mixture into the saucepan with the stock and juice. Add salt and pepper as necessary. Add the half-and-half. Simmer for 20 minutes total.

Meanwhile, cook the pasta (see page xiii).

Add the pasta to the soup the last few minutes of cooking and serve.

Kansas Pasta with Squash and Corn

My first (and only) speeding ticket was in Kansas. Driving along the flat roads at night, looking out into the vast farmlands, I guess I got mesmerized. From those fields comes this recipe using Kansas squash and corn.

2 medium acorn squash
1 medium onion, chopped
4 cloves garlic
3 tablespoons extra-virgin olive oil
1 pound rigatoni
One 15-ounce can hominy, undrained
½ tablespoon light soy sauce
½ teaspoon dried summer savory
¼ teaspoon dried oregano
¾ cup leftover squash water
1 tablespoon honey
Salt to taste (optional)
Freshly ground black pepper to taste

SERVES 4 TO 6

Peel and clean the squash, and cut into 1- to 2-inch chunks. Boil in a large saucepan in water to cover for about 10 minutes.

In a large skillet, sauté the onion and garlic in the olive oil until the onion is translucent.

Meanwhile, cook the pasta (see page xiii).

Remove the squash, reserving ¾ cup liquid, and add to the skillet with the onion and garlic. Add the hominy, soy sauce, summer savory, oregano, the reserved liquid, honey, salt, and pepper. Cover and simmer for 12 to 15 minutes. Spoon over pasta and serve.

❧ Pasta with Idaho Potatoes

Idaho boasts of its famous potatoes, which you should use in this recipe. Remember, potatoes are high in vitamin C and potassium and a decent source of vitamin B$_6$ and dietary fiber, not to mention that they are delicious as well.

2 large Idaho baking potatoes, diced
1 small zucchini, chopped
1 medium red pepper, seeded and chopped
1 pound penne
2 cloves garlic
¼ cup extra-virgin olive oil
1 cup pasta water
¾ teaspoon dried thyme
¾ teaspoon dried basil
1 cup shredded cheddar cheese
Salt to taste (optional)
Freshly ground black pepper to taste
1 cup low-fat mayonnaise

SERVES 4 TO 6

In a large pasta pot, bring the water to a boil, then add the potatoes, zucchini, red pepper, and pasta.

Meanwhile, sauté the garlic in olive oil in a large skillet. Drain the pasta and vegetables, reserving one cup of the water, and add to the skillet; continue to sauté, and add the reserved water. Add the thyme, basil, cheese, salt, and pepper, and stir until the cheese is melted. Remove from the heat, stir in the mayonnaise, and mix thoroughly. Serve.

Florida Pasta with Avocados and Salsa

After California, Florida is the second largest avocado producer. It also offers a diverse culture of tastes.

1 pound radiators
1 large ripe avocado or 2 small avocados, peeled
1 cup low-fat sour cream
2 cloves garlic
1 tablespoon extra-virgin olive oil
1 small red onion, chopped
2 medium tomatoes, chopped
Juice of ½ lime
½ teaspoon Worcestershire sauce
½ teaspoon hot pepper sauce
Salt to taste (optional)
½ teaspoon white pepper
2 tablespoons fresh cilantro, chopped
½ cup shredded provolone cheese
½ cup pasta water

SERVES 4 TO 6

Cook the pasta (see page xiii). Reserve ½ cup of the pasta water when draining.

In a food processor or blender, purée the avocado with the sour cream.

In a medium skillet, sauté the garlic, onion, and tomatoes in the olive oil until the onions are translucent. Add the lime juice, Worcestershire sauce, hot pepper sauce, salt, pepper, and fresh cilantro. Add the avocado and sour cream mixture to the skillet and sauté over low heat. Add the cheese and pasta water, toss with the pasta, and serve.

California Vegetarian Pasta

I created this recipe years ago for a vegetarian friend from Los Angeles, who absolutely loved it.

1 pound twists
3 cloves garlic
½ cup extra-virgin olive oil
1 large red bell pepper, seeded and cut into 1-inch strips
1 large green zucchini, cut into ½-inch-thick slices
1 large red onion, sliced
6 plum tomatoes, chopped
4 ounces pitted black olives, sliced
1 teaspoon dried thyme
½ teaspoon dried basil
1 cup pasta water
Freshly ground black pepper to taste
Salt to taste (optional)

SERVES 4 TO 6

Cook the pasta (see page xiii). Reserve 1 cup of water when draining.
In a large skillet, sauté the garlic until it turns golden; discard the garlic. Add the pepper, zucchini, onion, tomatoes, olives, thyme, and basil. Sauté for about 20 minutes. Add the pasta water, pepper, and salt. Toss with the pasta and serve.

Pasta with Love

This is one of the most requested recipes in my repertoire. When I introduced this on Live with Regis & Kathie Lee *the response was overwhelming.*

12 ounces ziti or penne
2 bunches scallions, chopped
1 small red bell pepper, seeded and chopped
1 very large ripe tomato, chopped
½ cup extra-virgin olive oil
2 tablespoons drained capers
2 tablespoons chopped fresh basil (or 1 tablespoon dried basil)
Approximately 2 cups (low-fat or nonfat) ricotta cheese
Freshly ground black pepper to taste
Salt to taste (optional)
4 ounces low-fat or nonfat shredded mozzarella cheese

SERVES 4

Cook the pasta (see page xiii).

Meanwhile, in a medium saucepan, sauté the scallions, red pepper, and tomato in the olive oil until soft. Add the capers and basil and continue stirring. Add the ricotta, pepper, and salt. (If a smooth sauce is desired, put the ricotta through a fine strainer or sieve before adding to the pan.) Simmer until all the ingredients are blended together.

Divide the pasta among 4 plates and top with the sauce. Sprinkle with mozzarella and serve immediately.

❧ Speedway Cold Pasta Salad

While shooting a video in Charlotte, at the NASCAR motor speedway, and watching all the fans tailgating, I came up with this delicious cold pasta salad.

1 pound tricolor fusilli
2 cups low-fat or nonfat mayonnaise
1 teaspoon sugar
1 medium red onion, chopped
2 tablespoons Dijon mustard
½ cup sweet pickle relish
½ cup chopped mild chilies
4 hard-boiled egg whites, chopped
Salt to taste (optional)
Freshly ground black pepper to taste

SERVES 4 TO 6

Cook the pasta (see page xiii), drain, rinse well, and place in the refrigerator until cool.

Meanwhile, in a large bowl, combine the mayonnaise, sugar, onion, mustard, relish, and chilies and mix in the pasta. Add the egg whites, salt, and pepper. Serve.

Pasta with Poultry

Chicken and turkey are great low-fat meat choices to be paired with pasta. A little goes a long way and with the addition of selected ingredients, such as chickpeas, as in my West Virginia Pasta, an economical dish can be made expansive in taste.

Southwestern Chicken and Chile Pasta with only one whole chicken breast serves up a lot of flavor, but is tame enough for everyone to enjoy.

Pasta with Spanish-flavored Spicy Chicken

A trip to Spain inspired this earthy, quick, and delicious dish.

1 pound skinless and boneless chicken, cut into 1-inch pieces
3 tablespoons extra-virgin olive oil
4 cloves garlic, chopped
1 medium onion, chopped
1 medium red bell pepper, chopped
½ teaspoon ground turmeric
2 cups chicken stock
One 28-ounce can crushed tomatoes
½ teaspoon dried oregano
½ teaspoon dried thyme
¼ teaspoon crushed red pepper
Salt to taste (optional)
Freshly ground black pepper to taste
1 pound fettuccine

SERVES 4 TO 6

In a large skillet, brown the chicken in the olive oil. Add the garlic, onion, bell pepper, and turmeric, and sauté briefly. Add the chicken stock, tomatoes, oregano, thyme, crushed red pepper, salt, and pepper. Cover and simmer for 20 to 30 minutes.

Meanwhile, cook the pasta (see page xiii). Serve the sauce over the pasta.

Southwestern Chicken and Chile Pasta

The flavor of the Southwest is served up with love!

1 whole chicken breast, skinless and boneless
2 tablespoons extra-virgin olive oil
1 medium onion, diced
1 red bell pepper, diced
2 tablespoons diced canned green chilies, undrained
2 cloves garlic, chopped
¾ teaspoon chili powder
½ teaspoon ground cilantro
1 cup chicken stock
1 cup light cream or half-and-half
Salt to taste (optional)
Freshly ground black pepper to taste
½ cup fresh cilantro, chopped plus whole sprigs for garnish
1 pound ziti or penne

SERVES 4 TO 6

In a large skillet, sauté the chicken in the olive oil. When the chicken is cooked, remove and set aside. In the same skillet, sauté the onion, bell pepper, chili, and garlic. Cut the chicken into bite-size pieces, return to the skillet, and add the chili powder, ground cilantro, chicken stock, cream, salt, and pepper. Add the fresh cilantro. Stir and simmer until the liquid is reduced by two thirds.

Meanwhile, cook the pasta (see page xiii).

Spoon the sauce over the pasta, garnish with sprigs of fresh cilantro, and serve.

Tennessee Pasta with Chicken and Bourbon

The birthplace of bourbon gives this sauce its smooth and mellow flavor.

2 tablespoons unsalted butter
2 large chicken breasts, halved, skinned, and boned
½ cup sour mash or bourbon
4 to 6 shallots, sliced
1 pound fettuccine
½ cup chicken stock
½ cup heavy cream
⅛ teaspoon ground nutmeg
1 tablespoon flour
¼ teaspoon white pepper
Salt to taste (optional)

SERVES 4 TO 6

In a medium skillet, heat the butter over high heat and cook the chicken on both sides until brown. Sprinkle ¼ cup bourbon over the chicken and ignite it. Add the shallots and cook until the flames go out. Add the remaining bourbon and turn the chicken. Cover the skillet and cook over low heat for 12 to 15 minutes, or until the chicken is done. Remove the chicken, cut into strips, and set aside.

Meanwhile, cook the pasta (see page xiii).

Defat the pan juices in the skillet, if necessary, and add the broth, cream, nutmeg, flour, pepper, and salt. Add the chicken to the sauce and simmer until the sauce thickens.

In a large bowl, combine the pasta and the sauce, and toss well. Serve.

Farfalle and Chicken in Lemon Sauce

1 tablespoon unsalted butter
1 tablespoon extra-virgin olive oil
2 tablespoons all-purpose flour
1 cup chicken stock
¾ cup heavy cream
1 cup low-fat milk
Juice of 2 lemons
1 tablespoon chopped lemon zest
1 tablespoon capers, rinsed
¼ teaspoon white pepper
Salt to taste (optional)
1 whole skinned and boned chicken breast, cooked and cut into strips
1 pound farfalle

SERVES 4 TO 6

In a large skillet, heat the butter in the olive oil, stir in the flour, and cook until golden. Whisk in the chicken stock, and add the cream, milk, lemon juice, lemon zest, capers, pepper, and salt.

Stir and reduce over high heat, about 15 minutes, and add the chicken during the last 5 minutes of cooking.

Meanwhile, cook the pasta (see page xiii). Drain well, and toss the pasta with the sauce. Serve.

Fettuccine with Duck, Olives, and Mushrooms

This is a dish worth the time that it takes to prepare with love.

One 4- to 5-pound duck
1 tablespoon extra-virgin olive oil
1 tablespoon unsalted butter
1 medium onion, finely chopped
1 medium carrot, finely chopped
½ cup dry white wine
2 bay leaves
1 tablespoon chopped Italian parsley
½ teaspoon dried thyme
Freshly ground black pepper to taste
Salt to taste (optional)
18 green olives, pitted and sliced
1 cup chicken stock
1 pound fettuccine
¼ pound mushrooms, sliced

SERVES 4 TO 6

If you are using a frozen duckling, defrost it in the refrigerator overnight. Using a large, heavy knife, cut the duckling in half lengthwise through the breastbone and backbone. Cut the legs from the body, and separate the drumsticks from the thighs. Cut off the wings and discard them. Cut the breast halves across into 2 pieces, cutting off and discarding the attached backbone. You will now have 8 pieces of duckling.

Trim away any excess fat. Wash the pieces and pat them dry.

Put the duck pieces in a large skillet, skin side down. Cover and cook over low heat without any oil for 15 to 20 minutes. Remove the duck and discard the rendered fat.

In the same skillet, heat the oil and butter and sauté the onion and carrot for about 2 minutes. Add the wine and scrape the bottom of the skillet to loosen the browned bits. Return the browned duckling pieces to the skillet and add the bay leaves, parsley, thyme, pepper, salt, olives, and broth. Cover and cook for 20 to 30 minutes.

Cook the pasta (see page xiii).

Add the mushrooms to the skillet and check the seasonings. You may need another ½ teaspoon thyme or more pepper and salt. Continue cooking for about 20 minutes, until the juices run clear when the duck is pricked with a fork. Turn off the heat. Remove the duckling from the pan and bone all duck pieces. Return to the pan and stir-fry for 1 minute. Remove the bay leaves, toss with the pasta, and serve.

North Carolina Pasta with Yams

Yams originated in Africa and their cousins, sweet potatoes, were born in the South. Both boast of containing antioxidants, beta carotene, vitamin C, and plenty of flavor!

1 pound shells
3 medium yams, peeled and halved
½ pound turkey sausage, casing removed
3 tablespoons extra-virgin olive oil
1 small onion, chopped
½ teaspoon celery seeds
⅛ teaspoon pumpkin pie spice
1 cup chicken stock
Salt to taste (optional)
Freshly ground black pepper to taste
One 10-ounce package chopped frozen spinach

SERVES 4 TO 6

Cook the pasta (see page xiii) and save the pasta water.

Add the yams to the same boiling water in which the pasta was cooked. Remove yams after about 16 minutes, or when they show a slight resistance to piercing with a fork. Let cool.

Meanwhile, in a large skillet, sauté the sausage meat in 1 tablespoon of olive oil. Separate meat into pieces with a spoon as it cooks. Remove the meat with a slotted spoon and set aside. Discard the fat remaining in the skillet.

Cut the yams into cubes and sauté them with the onion in a skillet in the remaining 2 tablespoons of olive oil. When the onion is translucent, add the celery seeds, pumpkin pie spice, chicken stock, salt, and pepper. Add the cooked sausage meat and spinach, cover, and simmer for 15 minutes. Then add the pasta to the skillet and mix together thoroughly. Serve.

Massachusetts Cold Pasta Salad
with Cranberries

The state that gives us cranberries was the inspiration for this flavor-infused recipe.

1 pound twists
2 cups low-fat mayonnaise
8 ounces cranberry sauce
½ teaspoon ground dried cilantro
¼ teaspoon white pepper
Salt to taste (optional)
1 small carrot, diced
2 celery ribs, thinly sliced
1 small red onion, chopped
12 ounces cooked turkey, cut into cubes

SERVES 4 TO 6

Cook the pasta (see page xiii). Rinse, drain well, and cool.

In a medium bowl, add the mayonnaise, cranberry sauce, cilantro, white pepper, salt, carrot, celery, and onion. Mix in the pasta and turkey. Refrigerate for a few hours before serving.

Ohio Pasta with Turkey and Beans

In the many years I have been making guest appearances on Cincinnati TV and radio shows, I am astonished by the many local chili parlors, serving it many ways.

1 pound ground turkey
3 tablespoons extra-virgin olive oil
1 medium onion, sliced
1 small green pepper, chopped
2 cups tomato sauce
One 15-ounce can pinto beans or chili beans, undrained
½ teaspoon dried cumin
1 teaspoon dried oregano
½ teaspoon chili powder
Hot pepper sauce to taste
½ teaspoon sugar
Salt to taste (optional)
1 pound spaghetti, broken into 3-inch pieces

SERVES 4

In a large skillet, sauté the turkey in 1 tablespoon of olive oil until it browns. Remove and set aside, discarding the fat.

Add the remaining 2 tablespoons of olive oil to the same skillet, and sauté the onions and green pepper until the onions are translucent. Add the tomato sauce, beans, cumin, oregano, chili powder, hot pepper sauce, sugar, and salt. Return the browned turkey to the skillet, cover, and simmer for about 35 minutes.

Meanwhile, cook the pasta (see page xiii). Spoon the chili over the pasta and serve.

Grandma's Chicken and Tomato Pasta

When I was a little guy, I often sat at my grandma's table and watched her put together this dish that was a family favorite. After jogging my memory and checking with Aunt Ida, I came up with a close variation.

2 large chicken breasts, skinned, boned, and cut into bite-size pieces
½ cup all-purpose flour
¼ cup extra-virgin olive oil
12 medium pitted olives, chopped
1 onion, chopped
One 16-ounce can plum tomatoes, chopped and undrained
½ teaspoon dried rosemary
1 tablespoon unsalted butter
½ pound mushrooms, sliced
¾ cup dry white wine
Freshly ground black pepper to taste
Salt to taste (optional)
1 pound rigatoni

SERVES 4 TO 6

Coat the chicken with the flour and brown the pieces in olive oil in a large skillet. Add the olives, onion, tomatoes, rosemary, butter, mushrooms, white wine, pepper, and salt. Cover, and simmer for 20 minutes, or until the chicken is thoroughly cooked.

Meanwhile, cook the pasta (see page xiii). Spoon the sauce over each portion of pasta and serve.

Chicken Pasta Pilaf

Years ago, when I first demonstrated this recipe on national television, we received thousands of requests—to date eight million requests have been filled. Enjoy!

1 cup thin spaghetti, uncooked and broken into 2-inch pieces
½ cup uncooked long-grain rice
⅓ cup extra-virgin olive oil
3 cups chicken stock
1 cup fresh or frozen and thawed broccoli florets
¼ teaspoon dried thyme, crushed
1 cup cooked chicken breast, cut into julienne strips
½ cup sliced scallions
¼ cup chopped walnuts
¼ cup diced red bell peppers

SERVES 4

In a medium saucepan, sauté the spaghetti and rice in olive oil until golden, stirring often. Add the chicken stock and bring to a boil. Add the broccoli and thyme. Cover and simmer 15 minutes, or until the rice is tender, stirring occasionally. Add the remaining ingredients and cook until heated through, stirring occasionally. Serve.

Tetrazzini

Try this and you will never buy the frozen variety again.

12 ounces fettuccine or eggless noodles
1 cup sliced mushrooms
3 tablespoons unsalted butter or margarine
2 tablespoons all-purpose flour
1¼ cups 1 percent low-fat milk
1 cup chicken stock
⅛ teaspoon ground nutmeg
⅛ teaspoon white pepper
⅛ teaspoon sweet paprika
1 large egg, beaten
¼ cup grated Parmesan cheese
1 cup frozen baby peas
2 cups cooked chicken or turkey cut into bite-size pieces
Salt to taste (optional)
½ cup chopped parsley

SERVES 4 TO 6

Cook the pasta (see page xiii).

In a medium skillet, sauté the mushrooms in the butter. Sprinkle in the flour and mix and cook the roux slowly until it turns golden. Add the milk and stock and stir well. Mix in the nutmeg, pepper, and paprika, and blend in the egg and cheese. Mix well, and add the peas, chicken or turkey, and salt. Simmer and stir for several minutes, until thick and creamy.

Put the pasta into a serving dish and spoon the cream sauce over the top. Garnish with the parsley and serve.

Pasta with Turkey Hash

To be enjoyed at breakfast, brunch, or while watching a late TV movie.

½ pound small elbows
1 cup turkey gravy
½ cup minced onion
½ cup thinly sliced celery
½ cup sliced mushrooms
3 generous pinches dried parsley flakes
Pinch freshly ground nutmeg
¼ teaspoon of ground rosemary
Dash hot pepper sauce
2 cups diced cooked turkey

SERVES 4 TO 6

Cook the pasta as usual (see page xiii).

In a medium skillet, heat the gravy and add the onion, celery, and mushrooms. Bring to a boil over medium-high heat, reduce the heat, and simmer for about 8 minutes.

Add the parsley flakes, nutmeg, rosemary, and hot pepper sauce. Add the pasta and turkey and blend thoroughly. Cook for another 5 minutes. Place in an ovenproof baking pan and broil the hash, until crisp on top. Serve.

Pasta with Turkey in Beer Sauce

Beer is a very popular beverage, and here I give you a flavor that rings all bells!

1 medium onion, chopped
¼ cup pimento, chopped
12 ounces smoked turkey kielbasa, chopped
1 tablespoon extra-virgin olive oil
¼ cup unsalted butter
¼ cup all-purpose flour
1 cup whole milk
1 cup half-and-half
¼ teaspoon ground turmeric
¼ teaspoon white pepper
1 teaspoon ground mustard
8 ounces cheddar cheese, shredded
¼ cup grated Romano cheese
12 ounces dark beer
Salt to taste (optional)
1 pound wagon wheels

SERVES 4 TO 6

In a small saucepan, sauté the onion, pimento, and kielbasa in the olive oil. In a medium saucepan, melt the butter and add the flour and sauté until it becomes a golden roux. Add the milk, cream, turmeric, pepper, and mustard, and whisk constantly on simmer. Add the cheeses and beer.

Add the mixture of onion, pimento, and kielbasa to the cheese sauce. Mix well and simmer for 12 to 15 minutes. Add the salt.

Meanwhile, cook pasta (see page xiii). Spoon the mixture over the pasta and serve.

~ Linguine with Chicken and Fennel

The anise-like fragrance of fennel and fennel seeds permeates the house when it is cooked—and it makes your mouth water.

2 tablespoons extra-virgin olive oil
2 medium to large chicken breasts, skinless, cut in half, and boneless
1 medium onion, chopped
2 cloves garlic, chopped
1 cup chicken stock
Juice of ½ lemon
1 teaspoon ground ginger
1 teaspoon ground turmeric
Salt to taste (optional)
Freshly ground black pepper to taste
1 teaspoon fennel seeds
¼ cup chopped Italian parsley
1 pound linguine

SERVES 4 TO 6

In a large skillet, heat the oil and cook the chicken until brown on both sides. Reduce the heat and add the onion and garlic. Cover and cook for 15 to 20 minutes.

Remove the chicken from the skillet, discarding any fat, and cut the chicken into thin strips. Return the chicken to the skillet and add the stock, lemon juice, ginger, turmeric, salt, pepper, and fennel seeds. Cover and cook until the chicken is done, about 15 minutes. Add the parsley.

Meanwhile, cook the pasta (see page xiii). In a large bowl, combine the chicken and pasta, and toss well. Serve.

Sweet and Sour Chicken with Fettuccine

When we think of our visits to the Chinese restaurant, we savor the combination of sweet-and-sour—here is the taste with pasta.

1 pound fettuccine
6 cloves garlic, sliced
1 bunch scallions, sliced
1 small red pepper, chopped
2 tablespoons extra-virgin olive oil
1 cup chicken stock
½ cup sugar
Salt to taste (optional)
1 teaspoon light soy sauce
½ cup white vinegar
1 teaspoon ground ginger
2 tablespoons cornstarch
Red food coloring, if desired
3 cooked chicken breasts, boneless, skinless, and cut into chunks

SERVES 4 TO 6

Cook the pasta (see page xiii).

In a large skillet, sauté the garlic, scallions, and red pepper in the olive oil until soft. Add the stock, sugar, salt, soy sauce, vinegar, ginger, cornstarch, and food coloring. Bring to a boil, reduce the heat to a simmer, add the chicken, and cook until heated through. Mix with the pasta and serve.

Pasta Stroganoff

Turkey fillets continue to be popular. This dish will soon be on your family's list of all-time favorites!

2 tablespoons extra-virgin olive oil
1 pound turkey fillets, cut into thin strips
One 10-ounce package frozen pearl onions
4 ounces mushrooms, sliced
1 cup chicken stock
One 10-ounce package frozen peas
½ teaspoon ground nutmeg
½ teaspoon white pepper
Salt to taste (optional)
1 pound fusilli
1 cup nonfat sour cream
½ cup pasta water

SERVES 4 TO 6

In a large skillet, sauté the turkey in olive oil, remove, and set aside. Add the onions and mushrooms and sauté until the onions are translucent. Add the stock and return the turkey to the skillet. Add the peas, nutmeg, pepper, and salt, and simmer, uncovered, for 20 to 30 minutes.

Meanwhile, cook the pasta (see page xiii). Reserve ½ cup of water when draining.

Add the sour cream to the skillet and stir together all ingredients (add pasta water, if needed). Toss with the pasta and serve.

Curry-style Noodles

Curry powder is a very personal selection. I prefer a full flavor but not too spicy and hot for this dish.

½ pound noodles
2 tablespoons unsalted butter
2 tablespoons all-purpose flour
2½ teaspoons curry powder
1 tablespoon fresh lemon juice
1 cup chicken stock
1 cup heavy cream
1 to 1½ pounds cooked turkey or chicken, cut into pieces

SERVES 4

Cook the pasta (see page xiii).

In a large skillet, heat the butter over low heat and blend in the flour to make a roux. Stir in the curry powder. Gradually blend in the lemon juice and stock, stirring constantly. Raise the heat to medium and continue cooking until the volume is reduced by half. Add the cream and cook until the mixture thickens.

Reduce the heat to low, add the turkey or chicken meat, and continue simmering for about 10 minutes. Toss with the noodles and serve.

Pasta with Smoked Turkey

You can buy pieces of cooked and packaged turkey meat or you can have your deli man cut one thick slice.

1 pound penne
3 tablespoons unsalted butter
8 ounces sliced, smoked deli turkey, ¼ inch thick, cut into strips
1 small onion, diced
6 plum tomatoes, diced
1 cup heavy cream
½ cup fresh or frozen peas
Freshly ground black pepper to taste
⅛ teaspoon ground nutmeg
¼ cup grated Parmesan cheese

SERVES 4 TO 6

Cook the pasta (see page xiii).

In a large skillet, heat the butter over medium heat. Add the turkey and onion and cook for 3 to 5 minutes, or until the onion is translucent. Stir in the tomatoes, and add the cream, peas, pepper, and nutmeg, until the mixture is slightly thickened, 3 to 5 minutes. Add the Parmesan cheese and mix thoroughly. Toss with the pasta and serve.

Chicken and Fettuccine for Easter

Easter dinner is traditionally a family affair. This delicate pasta is a proven favorite with everyone–from grandpa to the youngest child.

1 pound fettuccine
3 chicken breasts, boneless and skinless
½ cup all-purpose flour
2 tablespoons extra-virgin olive oil
2 tablespoons unsalted butter
1 medium onion, thinly sliced
3 cloves garlic
Juice of 2 lemons
1½ teaspoons sugar
Salt to taste (optional)
¼ teaspoon white pepper

SERVES 4 TO 6

Cook the pasta (see page xiii).

Dust the chicken with the flour and set aside. In a medium skillet, heat the oil and butter, and sauté the chicken, onion, and garlic until the chicken is done. Discard the garlic.

Remove the chicken and set aside. Add the lemon juice, sugar, salt, and pepper and stir until blended. Slice the chicken into thin strips, and return to the skillet. Stir for a minute or two to distribute the flavors evenly.

In a large bowl, combine the pasta with the chicken mixture. Toss well and serve.

❧ Cold Turkey for Labor Day

I rarely enjoy cold pasta, but this one is an exception! It's a rich creamy turkey salad with pasta.

1 pound orzo
Juice of ½ lemon
1 tablespoon lemon zest
2 ribs celery, thinly sliced
2 tablespoons Dijon mustard
2 cups low-fat mayonnaise
½ teaspoon dried rosemary
¼ teaspoon white pepper
Salt to taste (optional)
3 turkey fillets, cooked and cut into cubes (about 2 cups)

SERVES 4 TO 6

Cook the pasta (see page xiii), drain, rinse well, and cool in the refrigerator.

In a medium bowl, mix together the lemon juice, lemon zest, celery, mustard, mayonnaise, rosemary, pepper, and salt, and mix well. Add the orzo and turkey to the mixture. Refrigerate for a few hours before serving.

Pasta with Italian Sausage for the Super Bowl

This is great food for your tailgate party at home. Serve a simple feast for a day of TV with friends. A big fresh salad and crisp breadsticks are all you need to make it perfect.

1 pound spaghetti
½ pound Italian-style turkey sausage meat, casing removed
4 large eggs
4 egg whites
1 tablespoon extra-virgin olive oil
½ cup grated Parmesan cheese
½ tablespoon dried oregano
½ teaspoon white pepper
15 ounces ricotta cheese
1 cup shredded mozzarella cheese

SERVES 6 TO 8

Preheat the oven to 350°F. Grease a 9- × 9-inch square baking dish.
Cook the pasta (see page xiii).
In a large skillet, sauté the sausage meat. Drain and set aside.
In a large bowl, beat the eggs until foamy. Add the cooked pasta, sausage meat, olive oil, Parmesan cheese, oregano, and white pepper and mix thoroughly. Pour into the baking dish and bake at 350°F for 30 minutes. Remove from the oven and spread a layer of ricotta cheese on the pasta and top with the mozzarella cheese. Bake for an additional 15 to 20 minutes. Serve hot.

Pasta Hash for the Day After Thanksgiving

1 cup turkey gravy
½ cup minced onion
1 cup boiled potatoes, unpeeled and diced
½ cup thinly sliced celery
½ cup sliced mushrooms
¾ pound dumpling-style noodles
3 generous pinches dried parsley
Pinch freshly ground nutmeg
2 pinches dried rosemary
2 cups diced cooked turkey
½ cup heavy cream

SERVES 4 TO 6

In a medium saucepan, heat the gravy and add the onion, potatoes, celery, and mushrooms. Bring to a boil over medium-high heat, reduce the heat, and simmer for about 8 minutes.

Cook the pasta (see page xiii).

Preheat the broiler.

Add the parsley, nutmeg, and rosemary to the gravy. Add the turkey and stir thoroughly, cooking for another 5 minutes. Add the pasta and mix well. Put the mixture in an ovenproof baking dish, pour the cream over the top to cover, and broil until the top becomes crispy. Serve.

Fusilli with Spicy Chicken for New Year's Day

Spending New Year's Day at a friend's home in Wisconsin I decided to throw together a dinner from random items in her cupboard. A New Year's pasta dish was created.

1 medium onion, chopped
4 cloves garlic
3 tablespoons extra-virgin olive oil
1 large red pepper, chopped
2 whole chicken breasts, chopped
¾ cup dry white wine
1 teaspoon fennel seeds
1 teaspoon ground cumin
1 tablespoon hot pepper sauce
Freshly ground black pepper to taste
Salt to taste (optional)
1 pound fusilli
1 cup shredded Swiss cheese

SERVES 4 TO 6

In a medium skillet, sauté the onion and garlic in olive oil. Add the red pepper, chicken, and wine. Stir in the fennel seeds, cumin, hot pepper sauce, pepper, and salt, and stir for 20 minutes until well blended.

Cook the pasta (see page xiii).

In a large bowl, combine the pasta with the onion-garlic mixture and toss. Add the Swiss cheese and serve.

African Pasta

Although we did have a course on African cooking at my school, Cooking with Love, I recently put this together after watching Humphrey Bogart in the movie African Queen *for the twenty-fifth time—don't ask why!*

4 chicken cutlets
1 large onion, sliced
4 cloves garlic, minced
1 teaspoon hot pepper sauce
1 cup chicken stock
1 cup cider vinegar
¼ teaspoon ground dried cilantro
Salt to taste (optional)
Freshly ground black pepper to taste
2 bay leaves
3 tablespoons extra-virgin olive oil
1 pound fettuccine

SERVES 4 TO 6

In a 9- × 9-inch baking dish, put the chicken cutlets side by side. In a small bowl, mix the onion, garlic, hot pepper sauce, chicken stock, vinegar, cilantro, salt, pepper, and bay leaves. Pour the mixture over the chicken. Cover the dish with plastic wrap and refrigerate for several hours; turn the chicken once.

Remove the cutlets from the marinade, reserving the marinade for later use. In a large skillet, sauté the chicken on both sides in olive oil, until brown. Remove and cut into strips ½ inch × 3 inches thick and set aside. Add the marinade mixture to the skillet and cook over high heat, 12 to 15 minutes, to reduce by half.

Meanwhile, cook the pasta (see page xiii).

Reduce the heat to a simmer and add the chicken. Cover and continue to cook for about 20 minutes, or until the chicken is well done. Discard the bay leaves. Spoon the chicken over the pasta and serve.

West Virginia Pasta
with Turkey and Chickpeas

2 tablespoons extra-virgin olive oil

2 cloves garlic

1 pound turkey breast meat, cooked and diced

One 16-ounce can stewed tomatoes

One 16-ounce can chickpeas, undrained

2 cups chicken stock

2 tablespoons dried chives

½ teaspoon cayenne pepper

Juice of ½ lemon

1 tablespoon wine vinegar

Salt to taste (optional)

Freshly ground black pepper to taste

1 pound small shells

SERVES 4 TO 6

In a large skillet, sauté the garlic in the olive oil. When the garlic turns golden, discard it. Add the turkey, tomatoes, chickpeas, chicken stock, chives, cayenne pepper, lemon juice, vinegar, salt, and pepper, and simmer for 20 to 30 minutes.

Meanwhile, cook the pasta (see page xiii). Toss the ingredients with the pasta and serve.

Delaware Pasta

1 pound ziti
3 tablespoons extra-virgin olive oil
2 cloves garlic
1 bunch scallions, sliced
2 chicken breasts, boneless, skinless, and cut into strips
1 small red bell pepper, chopped
1 slice cooked ham, cut into ¼-inch-wide strips
½ cup chicken stock
1 cup heavy cream
¼ teaspoon ground turmeric
2 tablespoons Dijon mustard
One 10-ounce package frozen peas
½ cup grated Parmesan cheese
¼ teaspoon white pepper
Salt to taste (optional)

SERVES 4 TO 6

Cook the pasta (see page xiii). In a large skillet, sauté the garlic in olive oil until golden; discard the garlic. Add the scallions, chicken, bell pepper, and ham.

Cook for about 15 minutes or until the chicken is thoroughly cooked, remove, and set aside. Add the stock, and scrape the pan. Add the cream, turmeric, and mustard. Stir constantly and cook until it thickens, about 5 minutes. Add the peas, Parmesan cheese, pepper, and salt, and cook for 2 to 3 minutes. Toss with the pasta and serve.

Michigan Pasta with Turkey

Some people may prefer white meat ground turkey instead of the mixed variety. There's also less fat.

1 pound ground turkey
1 medium onion, peeled and chopped
1 green bell pepper, chopped
2 tablespoons extra-virgin olive oil
2 cups tomato sauce
½ teaspoon sugar
½ teaspoon dried oregano
1 teaspoon garlic powder
Salt to taste (optional)
Freshly ground black pepper to taste
1 pound medium elbows

SERVES 4 TO 6

In a large skillet, sauté the turkey, onion, and green pepper in olive oil. Cook until the meat is browned and the onions are translucent. Add the tomato sauce, sugar, oregano, garlic powder, salt, and pepper. Simmer, covered, for about 25 minutes.

Meanwhile, cook the pasta (see page xiii). Add the cooked pasta to the skillet, mix to combine, and serve.

Pasta with Meat

This is a collection of effortless, delicious dishes that can be made simply by giving leftovers a new name. For example, that baked ham which was carved for Sunday dinner can now be utilized for a creamy ham sauce on bow ties. That corned beef brisket can be shredded and teamed up with elbows, a few spices and barbecue sauce, and baked in a loaf pan for less than one hour. This makes a man-size *"Father's Day Loaf."*

Crisp bacon, partnered with cheddar cheese and shells and a few other simple ingredients, becomes a tantalizing casserole in 30 minutes. Double the recipe and you have a great *"Ball Game"* crowd pleaser.

Obviously, being chained to the kitchen stove is not what these time-saving, simple but elegant dishes are about.

The mix and variety of some of your family's favorite cuts of meat enhance the pasta and make you truly a "Love Chef"!!

Hearty Irish Pasta with Lamb

Years ago, while driving through the Irish countryside, I enjoyed many a bowl of great stew accompanied with pints of Guinness. Here I have replaced the potatoes with shells and found a great mix.

3 tablespoons extra-virgin olive oil
1 clove garlic, minced
1½ pounds lamb shoulder or boneless lamb for stew, cut into 1-inch cubes
½ teaspoon dried rosemary
½ teaspoon dried thyme
Freshly ground black pepper to taste
Salt to taste (optional)
1 cup water
1 cup beef stock
1 cup dry red wine
4 carrots, peeled and chopped
1 medium onion, chopped
2 ribs celery, chopped
1 pound medium shells
2 tablespoons flour stirred in 3 tablespoons water
2 tablespoons chopped fresh parsley

SERVES 4 TO 6

In a large Dutch oven, heat the oil and add the garlic. Sauté the garlic for 1 minute. Add the meat and brown on all sides in the hot oil. Add the rosemary, thyme, pepper, salt, water, beef stock, and red wine. Cover the pan and simmer 45 minutes to 1 hour, stirring occasionally.

Add the vegetables, cover, and cook 20 minutes longer, or until the meat and vegetables are tender.

Meanwhile, cook the pasta (see page xiii).

Add the flour-and-water mixture to thicken the sauce. Taste and add additional seasonings, if desired. Mix in the cooked pasta and sprinkle with chopped parsley. Serve hot.

Curried Lamb and Tomato Pasta

1 small onion, chopped
¼ cup extra-virgin olive oil
3 tablespoons curry powder
⅛ teaspoon cayenne pepper
1 tablespoon ground turmeric
Salt to taste (optional)
1½ pounds boneless lamb for stew, cut into ½-inch cubes
2 cups water
1 medium tomato, chopped
Juice of ½ lime
1 pound rigatoni

SERVES 4 TO 6

In a large skillet, sauté the onion in olive oil. Add the curry powder, cayenne pepper, turmeric, and salt and mix thoroughly. Cook until the onion is soft, add the meat and water, cover, and simmer for about 1½ hours. Add the tomato and lime juice, and cook for an additional 20 minutes.

Cook the pasta (see page xiii). Spoon the curried lamb over the pasta and serve.

Colorado Pasta with Lamb and Eggplant

Westerns often depict ranchers' hearty meals as comprised of beef or lamb, and beans. OK, so I threw in some eggplant!

1 pound ground lamb
2 tablespoons extra-virgin olive oil
2 cloves garlic, minced
1 small onion, sliced
2 cups tomato sauce or Marinara Sauce (see page 178)
1 cup water
1 medium eggplant, skin on, cubed (6 cups)
One 15-ounce can baked beans
½ teaspoon dried thyme
About ½ teaspoon dried basil
1 tablespoon grated Parmesan cheese
Freshly ground black pepper to taste
Salt to taste (optional)
½ pound large elbows
1 cup shredded mozzarella or Swiss cheese

SERVES 4 TO 6

In a large skillet, lightly brown the lamb in oil. Remove the lamb and sauté the garlic and onion in the drippings until the onion is translucent. Discard the excess fat.

Add the lamb, tomato sauce, water, eggplant, beans, thyme, basil, Parmesan cheese, pepper, and salt to the skillet. Cover and simmer 25 to 30 minutes, or until the lamb is tender.

Cook the pasta (see page xiii). Combine the pasta with the lamb mixture. Sprinkle the shredded cheese over the top and serve.

Couscous with Lamb

2 pounds lamb shoulder or boneless lamb for stew, cut into 1-inch cubes
2 tablespoons extra-virgin olive oil
2 cloves garlic, minced
½ teaspoon dried rosemary
½ teaspoon dried thyme
Freshly ground black pepper to taste
Salt to taste (optional)
2 cups water
1½ cups beef stock
1 cup dry red wine
6 carrots, cut into chunks
4 small whole onions, quartered
4 ribs celery, cut into pieces
10 ounces frozen peas
2 tablespoons flour stirred in 3 tablespoons water
Couscous (see Moroccan Couscous, page 175; omit the raisins)
2 tablespoons chopped Italian parsley

SERVES 6

In a large Dutch oven, brown the meat briskly in 1 tablespoon of olive oil. Discard any excess fat. Add the garlic and the remaining oil, and sauté. Add the rosemary, thyme, pepper, salt, water, stock, and wine. Cover and simmer for 45 minutes to 1 hour, stirring occasionally. Add the carrots, onions, and celery. Cover and cook for 30 minutes longer. During the last 15 minutes of cooking, add the peas and stir in the flour-and-water mixture.

Meanwhile, cook the couscous according to the recipe (see page 175). Create a ring of couscous on a large serving platter, and place the lamb and vegetables in the center. Sprinkle parsley over the center and serve.

Nevada Pasta

1 tablespoon extra-virgin olive oil

1 clove garlic, minced

1½ pounds lamb shoulder or boneless lamb for stew, cut into 1-inch
  cubes

½ teaspoon dried rosemary

½ teaspoon dried thyme

Freshly ground black pepper to taste

Salt to taste (optional)

2 cups water

1 cup beef stock

1 cup dry red wine

4 carrots, chopped

2 medium onions, peeled and sliced

2 ribs celery, sliced

2 tablespoons flour stirred in 3 tablespoons water

1 pound rigatoni

SERVES 4 TO 6

In a large Dutch oven, heat the oil and add the garlic. Sauté garlic for
1 minute, then add the meat, and brown on all sides. Add the rosemary,
thyme, pepper, salt, water, beef stock, and red wine. Cover the pan and
simmer for 45 minutes to 1 hour, stirring occasionally.

Add the carrots, onions, and celery. Cover and cook 30 minutes
longer, or until the meat and vegetables are tender. Add the flour and
water mixture to thicken and cook for several minutes.

Cook the pasta (see page xiii). Spoon the meat over the pasta and
serve.

Nebraska Pasta with Lamb Chops

Lamb is a popular commodity from Nebraska, and when I first made this recipe, it was for a barbecue segment on the Today show. Later, when adding it atop a dish of leftover fettuccine, I created this recipe.

6 large shoulder lamb chops
½ cup extra-virgin olive oil
1 tablespoon red wine vinegar
1 tablespoon grated onion
½ teaspoon dried rosemary
Salt to taste (optional)
2 medium zucchini, sliced
2 medium ripe tomatoes, sliced
1 pound fettuccine
2 tablespoons unsalted butter
Freshly ground black pepper to taste

SERVES 4 TO 6

Preheat the oven to 375°F.

Cut heavy-duty aluminum foil into 6 squares big enough to hold 1 lamb chop on one-half of each square, leaving 1 or 2 inches at the edges for folding. Place each chop in the center of each piece of foil. Mix together the oil, vinegar, onion, rosemary, and salt if desired. Brush each chop with some of the mixture. Place zucchini and tomato slices on top of the chops, and drizzle the vegetables with the remainder of the mixture.

Fold into individual packets. Bake at 375°F for 30 minutes or cook on the grill to desired degree of doneness, about 16 minutes for medium.

Cook the pasta (see page xiii). Toss with the butter and pepper. Arrange the pasta on individual plates, and add the lamb chops and vegetables in the center of each serving.

Arkansas Pasta

2 cloves garlic
1 medium onion, diced
1 red bell pepper, diced
Freshly ground black pepper to taste
3 tablespoons extra-virgin olive oil
3 cups cooked ham, chopped
2 cups tomato sauce
½ cup heavy cream
1 tablespoon sweet paprika
1 teaspoon dried thyme
Salt to taste (optional)
¼ teaspoon crushed red pepper
1 pound spaghetti

SERVES 4 TO 6

In a large skillet, sauté the garlic, onion, red bell pepper, and black pepper in olive oil until soft. Add the ham, briskly stirring until ham is browned. Add the tomato sauce, cream, and seasonings and simmer for 20 minutes.

Meanwhile, cook the pasta (see page xiii). Put the spaghetti in a serving bowl and spoon the sauce over the pasta, and serve.

Pasta with Ham and Collard Greens

Ham and greens are a traditional favorite—now pairing it with beans and bow ties makes it a regal dish.

2 pounds collard greens, cleaned, stalks removed, and chopped
4 cups water
1 tablespoon Dijon mustard
Juice of 1 lemon
1 pound bow ties
3 tablespoons extra-virgin olive oil
2 cloves garlic, chopped
1 medium onion, chopped
1 cup lean ham chunks
One 19-ounce can cannellini beans, undrained
A *few dashes hot pepper sauce*
Salt to taste (optional)
Freshly ground black pepper to taste
1 cup pasta water

SERVES 4 TO 6

In a large saucepan, cook the greens in 4 cups of water which you bring to a boil. Cover and simmer for 40 minutes. Drain the water and reserve it to cook the pasta. Put the greens in a large bowl and mix the mustard and lemon juice together. Toss with the greens.

Cook the pasta (see page xiii). Reserve 1 cup of the pasta water when draining.

Meanwhile, in a large skillet, sauté the garlic, onion, and ham in the olive oil until the onion is translucent. Add the beans, pepper sauce, salt, pepper, and pasta water. Simmer for 8 to 10 minutes and add the greens. Toss with the pasta and serve.

Wisconsin Pasta with American Cheese and Ham

From the "Land of Cheese," this is a crowd pleaser. Bake a few dishes to bring to your tailgate parties and bring some seeded Italian bread!

½ *pound lasagna noodles*
2 *tablespoons extra-virgin olive oil*
1 *pound cooked ham, thinly sliced*
2 *red bell peppers, seeded and thinly sliced*
Freshly ground black pepper to taste
Salt to taste (optional)
½ *pound American cheese slices*
2 *large ripe tomatoes, thinly sliced*

SERVES 4 TO 6

Cook the pasta (see page xiii).

Preheat the oven to 350°F. Grease a 13- × 9- × 2-inch baking dish.

Place a layer of pasta on the bottom, add the olive oil, top with ham, then pepper slices, pepper, and salt. Repeat with a layer of pasta and top with the cheese and tomato slices. Bake at 350°F for about 30 minutes, or until the cheese is bubbly. Serve hot.

Alabama Pasta with Corn and Ham

1 medium onion, chopped
1 red bell pepper, seeded and chopped
One 10-ounce package frozen lima beans
1 thick (½-inch) slice ham, chopped
2 tablespoons extra-virgin olive oil
One 15¼-ounce can corn kernels, dry-packed, or kernels from 3 ears
    of corn
½ cup chicken stock
8 ounces orzo
1 teaspoon ground turmeric
1 teaspoon crushed red pepper
Salt to taste (optional)
Freshly ground black pepper to taste

SERVES 4 TO 6

In a large skillet, sauté the onion, bell pepper, lima beans, and ham in olive oil until the vegetables are soft. Add the corn, chicken stock, and sauté for 2 to 4 minutes.

Meanwhile, cook the pasta (see page xiii).

Add the turmeric, crushed red pepper, salt, and pepper. Add the cooked orzo to the skillet and stir to combine well. Serve.

⚛ Pasta Carbonara

This creamy and dreamy dish I enjoyed in a little restaurant I happened upon in Venice during a rainstorm—you can easily duplicate it in your kitchen.

1 pound vermicelli
1 cup chopped lean ham
2 tablespoons extra-virgin olive oil
2 jumbo eggs, coddled
½ cup grated Romano cheese
Freshly ground black pepper to taste
2 tablespoons unsalted butter
½ cup pasta water

SERVES 4 TO 6

Cook the pasta (see page xiii). Reserve ½ cup pasta water when draining.

In a large skillet, sauté the ham in the olive oil until crisp. In a mixing bowl, combine the eggs, cheese, and pepper and mix well.

Toss the pasta with the butter, add the egg mixture, and toss again. Spoon the pasta into the skillet with the ham and quickly sauté, stirring to combine. Add the pasta water and more pepper to taste. Serve immediately.

Louisiana Pasta with Spicy Shrimp and Sausage

Creating a pasta that represents Louisiana was easy—when you eat it, you will be reminded of "The Big Easy"!

½ pound andouille or kielbasa sausage, chopped
2 tablespoons extra-virgin olive oil
2 cloves garlic, minced
1 medium onion, chopped
One 16-ounce can stewed tomatoes
1 small green bell pepper, seeded and chopped
2 ribs celery, chopped
1¼ to 1½ pounds chicken cutlets, cut into 1-inch cubes
1 bay leaf
¼ teaspoon cayenne pepper
½ teaspoon dried thyme
1 pound large elbows
1 cup chicken stock
½ pound small shrimp, peeled and deveined
Salt to taste (optional)
Freshly ground black pepper to taste

SERVES 4 TO 6

In a large skillet, sauté the sausages in olive oil until crisp, about 6 minutes. Add the garlic and onion and cook an additional 2 minutes, until the onions are translucent. Add the tomatoes to the skillet with the green pepper, celery, and chicken. Season with bay leaf, cayenne pepper, and thyme. Stir and reduce the heat to a simmer.

Cook the pasta (see page xiii).

Add the chicken stock to the skillet, cover, and simmer about 30 minutes. During the last 10 minutes, add the shrimp and cooked pasta. Mix to combine, add the salt and pepper, and remove the bay leaf. Serve immediately.

Polish Pasta with Kielbasa Sausage

1 pound medium shells
1 pound regular or low-fat kielbasa sausage, sliced ¼ inch thick
1 medium onion, sliced
4 cloves garlic, whole
2 tablespoons extra-virgin olive oil
One 16-ounce can cannellini beans
3 tablespoons ketchup
¼ teaspoon dried oregano
Freshly ground black pepper to taste
Salt to taste (optional)
½ cup pasta water

SERVES 4 TO 6

Cook the pasta (see page xiii). Reserve ½ cup water when draining.

In a large skillet, sauté the sausage, onions, and garlic in the olive oil until the onions are soft. Add the beans, ketchup, oregano, pepper, and salt, cover, and continue to sauté. Add the pasta water to the skillet and mix. Toss the mixture with the pasta and serve.

North Dakota Pasta
with Sausage and Cabbage

1 small cabbage, roughly chopped
1 medium onion, chopped
¼ cup extra-virgin olive oil
½ teaspoon paprika
1 tablespoon caraway seeds
2 bay leaves
½ pound ziti
1 pound kielbasa sausage, thinly sliced
1 cup sour cream
Salt to taste (optional)
Freshly ground black pepper to taste

SERVES 4 TO 6

In a large skillet, sauté the cabbage and onion in olive oil. Add the paprika, caraway seeds, and bay leaves.

Cook the pasta (see page xiii).

Remove the bay leaves, and add the sausage and sour cream and mix well. Toss with the pasta, season with salt and pepper, and serve.

Iowa Pasta with Pork and Asparagus

The other "white meat" is a versatile partner for many ingredients, as most Iowa farmers know.

1 pound spaghetti
1¼ to 1½ pounds pork fillets, cut into ½- × 3-inch strips
½ cup all-purpose flour
3 tablespoons extra-virgin olive oil
3 cloves garlic
1 red pepper, seeded and chopped
½ pound fresh asparagus, peeled and cut into 3-inch pieces
Juice of ½ lemon
1 cup chicken stock
Salt to taste (optional)
Freshly ground black pepper to taste
⅓ cup toasted sesame seeds

SERVES 4 TO 6

Cook the pasta (see page xiii).

Coat the pork strips with flour. In a large skillet, sauté the pork in the olive oil until cooked. Remove and set aside. Defat the pan, if necessary. Add the garlic, and cook until golden; discard the garlic. Add the red pepper, sauté for 2 to 3 minutes, and add the asparagus, lemon juice, stock, salt, and pepper. Toss the vegetable mixture with the pasta. Place several pieces of pork on top of each serving and sprinkle with sesame seeds. Serve hot.

Autumn Harvest Pork and Apple Pasta

Picking apples in autumn in New York state was always a memorable time—the fragrant combination of apples, pork, and my favorite spice, cilantro, fills the kitchen.

4 pork fillets
1 tablespoon extra-virgin olive oil
1 tablespoon butter
Freshly ground black pepper to taste
1 small onion, thinly sliced
1 small tart apple, peeled, cored, and thinly sliced
1 tablespoon celery seeds
1 teaspoon ground cilantro
1 cup apple juice
1 tablespoon firmly packed brown sugar
½ pound medium noodles
Salt to taste (optional)

SERVES 4

In a large skillet, sauté the pork in the olive oil and butter for about 6 minutes on each side, until cooked. Remove and cut the pork into strips. Return to the skillet and add the pepper and onion over the pork. Put the apple, celery seeds, and cilantro on top of the onion, and pour in the apple juice. Sprinkle the brown sugar over all. Simmer, covered, for 40 minutes.

Meanwhile, cook the pasta (see page xiii). Stir the pork mixture and toss with the pasta. Add the salt and serve.

Arizona Pasta

1 1/2 pounds lean pork cutlets, cut into 1/2-inch cubes
2 tablespoons extra-virgin olive oil
1 medium onion, chopped
6 ripe plum tomatoes, chopped
2 cloves garlic, minced
1/2 teaspoon dried oregano
1/2 teaspoon ground cumin
1 tablespoon chili powder
1 bay leaf
Juice of 1/2 lemon
1/2 cup chopped fresh cilantro
Freshly ground black pepper to taste
Salt to taste (optional)
1 pound penne or ziti
1 cup pasta water

SERVES 4 TO 6

In a large skillet, sauté the pork cubes in olive oil. Remove the pork when cooked and set aside. Degrease the pan, if necessary.

Sauté the onion, and when soft, add the tomatoes, garlic, oregano, cumin, chili powder, and bay leaf. Let simmer, covered, for 20 minutes. Add the pork, lemon juice, fresh cilantro, pepper, and salt. Simmer, covered, for an additional 20 minutes, or until the pork is thoroughly cooked.

Meanwhile, cook the pasta (see page xiii). Reserve 1 cup pasta water when draining. Add the pasta water to the skillet and stir to combine. Remove the bay leaf. In a large bowl, combine the pasta and the pork mixture. Toss well and serve.

German Pasta

In a Munich beer garden, I enjoyed some "German Soul Food," washed down with steins of beer. On returning home, I concocted this dish in tribute.

Six 4-ounce pork cutlets
½ cup all-purpose flour
2 tablespoons extra-virgin olive oil
1 medium onion, peeled and chopped
4 cloves garlic, peeled and chopped
One 12-ounce can regular beer
One 10-ounce package frozen Brussels sprouts, halved
1 teaspoon caraway seeds
1 bay leaf
¼ teaspoon ground cilantro
Freshly ground black pepper to taste
Salt to taste (optional)
1 cup beef stock
1 pound fettuccine or noodles

SERVES 6 TO 8

Dust the pork cutlets with flour. In a large skillet, sauté the pork in the olive oil, and add the onions and garlic. Cook until the pork is browned on all sides; slice the pork into strips and set aside.

Meanwhile, add the beer to the skillet, scrape the pan and over high heat reduce to half the volume. Add the Brussels sprouts, caraway seeds, bay leaf, cilantro, pepper, salt, and beef stock. Simmer for 20 minutes.

Meanwhile, cook the pasta (see page xiii). Return the pork to the skillet and heat through. Toss with the pasta and serve.

Utah Pasta with Steak and Potatoes

1 pound beef flank steak, cut into ¼-inch-thick strips
2 tablespoons extra-virgin olive oil
1 pound rigatoni
1 medium sweet potato, peeled and diced
2 red peppers, cut into strips
1 medium onion, chopped
2 cloves garlic, chopped
1 cup chicken stock
1 teaspoon ground cumin
1 tablespoon ground ginger
1 teaspoon crushed red pepper
Salt to taste (optional)
Freshly ground black pepper to taste
1 cup pasta water

SERVES 4 TO 6

In a large skillet, sauté the beef in olive oil until browned on both sides; remove and set aside.

Meanwhile, cook the pasta (see page xiii) and the sweet potato. Reserve 1 cup of water when draining.

Add the peppers, onion, and garlic to the skillet and sauté and when the onions are translucent add the cooked pasta and sweet potato. Add the chicken stock, cumin, ginger, crushed red pepper, salt, and pepper. Mix well and sauté, adding the pasta water. Spoon over each serving of pasta.

Chili con Carne with Spaghetti

Pasta adds a natural "bulk" to one of my favorite chilis. Stretching the recipe, you may want to double the chili and freeze half of it. When thawing, cook up fresh spaghetti to mix with it. This is the original recipe I introduced on Live with Regis & Kathie Lee.

1 pound chuck steak
1 tablespoon all-purpose flour
4 tablespoons extra-virgin olive oil
1/2 large onion, sliced
1/2 cup red wine
1/2 cup tomato sauce
1 clove garlic, pressed
1/2 carrot, cut into matchsticks
1/2 green bell pepper, seeded and diced
One 10½-ounce can kidney beans, drained
One 10½-ounce can chickpeas, drained
One 10½-ounce can lentil soup
1 bay leaf
1/2 teaspoon ground cumin
1/2 teaspoon dried oregano
1/4 teaspoon crushed red pepper or to taste
Freshly ground black pepper to taste
1/2 pound spaghetti, broken into 2-inch pieces
Grated cheddar cheese (optional)

SERVES 4 TO 6

❧

Cut the steak into thin strips and sprinkle with the flour. In a very large skillet, heat 2 tablespoons of oil. Sauté the onion slices in the oil until translucent; remove the onion and set aside. Brown the meat in 2 batches in the hot oil, adding the remaining oil as needed.

Add 1/4 cup wine, and deglaze the skillet by scraping the browned bits from the bottom of the skillet and stirring. Add the tomato sauce, the onion, the remaining wine, and all the other ingredients, except the spaghetti and cheese. Taste and adjust seasonings.

Cover and cook over low heat for about 1½ hours, or until the meat is tender. Uncover for the last 30 minutes if the sauce needs thickening.

Cook the pasta (see page xiii). For each serving, combine equal portions of pasta and chili. Top with grated cheese, if desired, and serve.

Pasta with Meat Sauce

1 recipe meatballs (see page 116)
1 pound lean round steak, ground
6 sweet Italian sausages
¼ cup extra-virgin olive oil
1 small onion, chopped
2 cloves garlic
One 35-ounce can Italian plum tomatoes, undrained
3 ounces (6 tablespoons) tomato paste
3 ounces (6 tablespoons) water
1 teaspoon salt
Generous pinch of dried basil
1 pinch of dried thyme
Freshly ground black pepper to taste
1 pound rigatoni

SERVES 4 TO 6

In a large skillet, sauté the meatballs, ground beef, and sausages briefly in a little of the olive oil; drain off the fat.

Meanwhile, in another skillet, sauté the onion and garlic in the remaining oil for about 5 minutes. Chop the tomatoes coarsely, and add the tomatoes with the juices to the skillet. Add the tomato paste, water, salt, basil, thyme, and pepper and simmer, covered, for 30 minutes.

Add the meat to the sauce and cook, covered, an additional 30 minutes. Remove the cover, stir, and cook another 20 to 25 minutes.

In the meantime, cook the pasta (see page xiii). When it's ready, pour the sauce over the pasta and serve.

Pasta Paprikash

We use eggless noodles and nonfat sour cream here, yet this is a dish that is still big on taste!

2 pounds lean sirloin steak, cut into thin strips (discard fat)
2 tablespoons extra-virgin olive oil
2 medium onions, chopped
3 garlic cloves, minced
1 teaspoon Worcestershire sauce
4 teaspoons sweet paprika
3 cups tomato sauce
1 cup water
1 pound button mushrooms
1 tablespoon caraway seeds
1 pound eggless noodles
1 cup nonfat sour cream
Salt to taste (optional)
½ cup chopped Italian parsley

SERVES 4 TO 6

In a large skillet, brown the beef in olive oil. Remove the beef and set aside, and defat if necessary.

Add the onions to the skillet and cook until almost translucent. Add the garlic and continue to sauté for 1 to 2 minutes more. Add the Worcestershire sauce, paprika, and tomato sauce, and return the beef to the skillet. Cover, and cook for 1 hour. Add the water, mushrooms, and caraway seeds, and simmer for an additional 30 minutes.

Meanwhile, cook the pasta (see page xiii). Stir the sour cream and salt into the sauce. Put the noodles on a large serving platter. Spoon the beef sauce over top, sprinkle with parsley, and serve.

Illinois Pasta with Steak

Historically, Chicago has been the center of the meat-processing industry. The major cattleman's association and meat industry information agencies are still housed in Chicago.

1½ to 2 pounds round steak, lean
½ cup all-purpose flour
2 tablespoons extra-virgin olive oil
2 medium onions, chopped
1 tablespoon Worcestershire sauce
One 16-ounce can crushed tomatoes
¾ cup dry red wine
1 tablespoon dried sage
Freshly ground black pepper to taste
Salt to taste (optional)
1 pound rigatoni
1 cup pasta water
2 scallions, sliced

SERVES 4 TO 6

To tenderize the steak, pound it gently with a meat mallet. Coat the meat with flour.

In a large skillet, heat the olive oil and sauté the steak on both sides. Remove the steak and cut into bite-size strips; set aside. Add the onion and Worcestershire sauce to the skillet and sauté until the onions are transparent. Add the tomatoes, wine, sage, pepper, and salt, and return the steak to the skillet. Cover and simmer for 1¾ to 2 hours.

Cook the pasta (see page xiii). Reserve one cup of the pasta water when draining, and add to the skillet. Toss the steak with the pasta, and garnish with the scallions. Serve.

Indonesian Satay Pasta

The kabob, a popular staple at cocktail parties, is a popular food in Indonesia. The "satay" is usually meat grilled on a skewer, and dipped in or brushed with a delicious peanut sauce. Here, I have duplicated the taste with my pasta dressing.

1¼ to 1½ pounds beef sirloin, cut into cubes
1 tablespoon extra-virgin olive oil
1 small onion, chopped
1 medium green pepper, seeded and chopped
1 pound penne
¼ cup light soy sauce
¼ cup teriyaki sauce
¼ cup brown sugar
Juice of ½ lemon
¼ teaspoon ground cayenne pepper
¼ cup teaspoon white pepper
1 cup vanilla yogurt
¾ cup creamy peanut butter

SERVES 4 TO 6

In a medium skillet, sauté the steak in the olive oil until done. Add the onion and green pepper. Remove when cooked and set aside.

Meanwhile, cook the pasta (see page xiii).

Put the soy sauce, teriyaki sauce, brown sugar, lemon juice, and peppers into the skillet, and mix well; add the yogurt and peanut butter, and stir. Simmer and continue stirring for 4 to 6 minutes. Add the beef, onions, and pepper to the mixture, heat through, and toss with the cooked pasta. Serve.

Pasta with Texas-style Barbecued Ribs

My many visits to Texas always bring me to one of the many famous barbecue restaurants. I love barbecue so much, I just had to work out my own interpretation.

2 pounds lean beef short ribs
2 red bell peppers, seeded and sliced
1 cup red wine
2 cups tomato sauce
1 teaspoon Worcestershire sauce
1 medium onion, chopped
4 cloves garlic, minced
1 teaspoon chili powder
½ teaspoon ground cumin
1 tablespoon dark brown sugar
2 bay leaves
Freshly ground black pepper to taste
1 pound penne

Preheat the oven to 350°F.

In a large stockpot, boil the water and add the ribs. Remove the ribs after 20 minutes and discard the water.

Put the ribs in a large ovenproof baking pan in one layer. Mix the bell peppers, red wine, tomato sauce, Worcestershire sauce, onion, garlic, chili powder, cumin, and brown sugar. Add the bay leaves and pepper. Pour the mixture over the ribs. Cover and bake the ribs at 350°F for 1½ to 2 hours.

Cook the pasta (see page xiii). Remove the ribs and remove the meat from the bones, and chop into pieces. Add the meat to the sauce and mix well. Spoon the sauce over the pasta and serve.

Pasta with Beef Barbecue Sauce

Give me a barbecued, smoky taste and you're giving me love; add pasta and it's ecstasy.

1 small onion, chopped
1 teaspoon extra-virgin olive oil
2 pounds shredded cooked beef
1 teaspoon dark brown sugar
½ cup dry white wine
1 teaspoon Worcestershire sauce
1 cup ketchup
½ cup water
1 cup tomato sauce
1 clove garlic, minced
1 bay leaf
1 pound twists

SERVES 4 TO 6

In a medium saucepan, sauté the onion until it is translucent, about 5 minutes. Add the beef, and add the remaining ingredients, except the pasta, and simmer for 15 minutes.

Meanwhile, cook the pasta (see page xiii). Toss the sauce with the pasta and serve.

Pasta with Barbecue Pork Sauce: Substitute pork for shredded cooked beef, add a dash of Liquid Smoke, and cook as directed above.

Pasta with Kentucky Burgoo

Several years ago on Kentucky Derby Day, Live with Regis & Kathie Lee was produced live from Churchill Downs. On that show, I presented about eighteen dishes that were Kentuckian in origin. Among them was burgoo, a kind of stew that evolved over the years. Here, I represent Kentucky with my version.

4 chicken thighs
1 pound lean stew beef
2 quarts water
¼ cup extra-virgin olive oil
1 small onion, chopped
1 small green pepper, chopped
1 rib celery, sliced
1 cup sliced okra, fresh or frozen
1 cup corn kernels, canned or frozen
One 15-ounce can crushed tomatoes
1 cup canned butter beans
Juice of ½ lemon
¼ teaspoon crushed red pepper
⅛ teaspoon cayenne pepper
¼ teaspoon Worcestershire sauce
Freshly ground black pepper to taste
Salt to taste (optional)
1 pound ditalini

SERVES 6 TO 8

Put the chicken and beef in a large pot, add the water, cover the pot, and bring to a boil. Reduce the heat to a simmer and cook for about 2 hours.

Meanwhile, in a large skillet, sauté the onion, green pepper, and celery in the olive oil. Remove from the heat.

Strain the chicken and beef stock and defat, if necessary. Reduce the stock to 1 quart. When cool enough to handle, remove the chicken from the bone and shred the beef. Combine with the onion, pepper, and celery mix. Add the reduced stock, okra, corn, tomatoes, beans, lemon juice, red pepper, cayenne pepper, Worcestershire sauce, black pepper, and salt. Bring to a boil and reduce heat to a simmer. Cover, and cook for about 45 minutes.

Cook the pasta (see page xiii). Add to the stew and serve.

South Dakota Pasta with Beef

This beef-producing state prompted this unusual casserole that was a hit with all of our tasters.

1 pound elbows
1 tablespoon extra-virgin olive oil
1½ pounds ground lean beef
1 medium onion, chopped
¾ teaspoon chili seasoning
One 15-ounce can cream-style corn
4 ounces potato chips, crushed

SERVES 4 TO 6

❧

Preheat the oven to 350°F.

Cook the pasta (see page xiii).

In a medium skillet, sauté the meat in the olive oil until brown. Remove the meat, discard the fat, add the onion, and sauté.

Put a layer of cooked pasta in an ovenproof baking dish; top with a layer of meat and onion. Repeat the layers until the ingredients are used up. Sprinkle the top with chili seasoning and smooth the corn on top. Sprinkle the potato chips on top.

Bake at 350°F for about 1 hour 15 minutes. Serve immediately.

Wyoming Pasta with Cheddar Cheese and Bacon

1 pound medium shells
½ pound lean bacon
2 cups low-fat milk
2 tablespoons cornstarch
10 ounces cheddar cheese, shredded
½ teaspoon white pepper
One 10-ounce package frozen baby peas
⅓ cup unflavored bread crumbs

SERVES 4 TO 6

Preheat the oven to 375°F. Grease an ovenproof baking dish and set aside.

Cook the pasta (see page xiii).

Meanwhile, sauté the bacon in a medium skillet until crispy. In a medium saucepan over low heat, combine the milk and cornstarch. Add the cheese and pepper. Stir until thick and the cheese has melted; add the peas.

Drain and discard the bacon fat and crumble the bacon, using the meaty pieces, and add to the cheese sauce. Put the pasta in the baking dish. Mix in the cheese sauce and top with the bread crumbs. Bake at 375°F for 30 minutes, or until bubbly and brown on top. Serve immediately.

Pasta with Tomatoes and Lima Beans

1 medium onion, chopped
2 tablespoons extra-virgin olive oil
One 16-ounce can plum tomatoes, undrained
4 slices well-done bacon, crumbled
1/2 teaspoon dried thyme
Salt to taste (optional)
Freshly ground black pepper to taste
One 10-ounce package frozen baby lima beans
1 pound cavatelli
1 cup pasta water
1/4 cup chopped Italian parsley
1/4 teaspoon crushed red pepper
Grated Parmesan cheese

SERVES 4 TO 6

In a large skillet, sauté the onions in the olive oil until they are translucent. Add the tomatoes, bacon, thyme, salt, and pepper. (Save some crumbled bacon for garnish.) Break apart the tomatoes with a spoon. Cover and simmer about 20 minutes.

Add the lima beans to the pasta water before cooking pasta, 5 to 7 minutes. Drain well, and add to the skillet. Meanwhile, cook the pasta (see page xiii). Reserve 1 cup pasta water when draining.

Stir and add 1 cup pasta water; continue to simmer for 4 to 5 minutes. Spoon the sauce on individual servings and top with crumbled bacon, parsley, crushed red pepper, and sprinkle on cheese.

Indiana Pasta with Corn and Bits of Bacon

Hoosiers love their fresh corn and especially when romanced with pinto beans and bits of real bacon, everyone can now enjoy my tribute to Indiana.

½ pound bacon, fat removed
1 pound angel hair
2 tablespoons extra-virgin olive oil
1 bunch scallions, sliced
3 ears corn, shucked
1 cup chicken stock
¼ teaspoon ground cilantro
Freshly ground black pepper to taste
Salt to taste (optional)
One 16-ounce can pinto beans, undrained

SERVES 4 TO 6

In a medium skillet, fry the bacon until crisp. Remove the strips and drain on paper towels. Crumble, using the meaty bits only. Set aside.

Cook the pasta (see page xiii).

Meanwhile, in a medium skillet, sauté the scallions in olive oil until translucent. Add the corn, chicken stock, cilantro, pepper, and salt. Simmer, covered, for 2 minutes then add beans and simmer for 4 to 6 minutes. Toss with the pasta and bacon bits. Serve.

❧ New Hampshire Pasta with Venison

Since deer are plentiful here, I have given this state its own recipe.

1½ *pounds venison steak*
2 *tablespoons extra-virgin olive oil*
1 *tablespoon unsalted butter*
2 *medium onions, chopped*
1 *small carrot, sliced*
1 *clove garlic*
½ *pound mushrooms, sliced*
1 *tablespoon dried sage*
½ *teaspoon dried marjoram*
1 *tablespoon balsamic vinegar*
Freshly ground black pepper to taste
Salt to taste (optional)
1 *cup beef stock*
1 *pound rigatoni*
1 *cup pasta water*
½ *cup chopped Italian parsley*

SERVES 4 TO 6

In a large skillet, brown the venison steak in olive oil on both sides. Remove and cut into bite-size strips; set aside.

Put the butter into the skillet and sauté the onions, carrot, and garlic until the onions are translucent. Add the mushrooms, sage, marjoram, balsamic vinegar, pepper, and salt. Return the meat to the skillet and add the beef stock. Simmer for 30 to 40 minutes.

Cook the pasta (see page xiii). Reserve 1 cup pasta water when draining and mix into the skillet. Spoon the mixture over individual pasta servings and garnish with parsley before serving.

Noodles with Liver and Onions

For all those who love liver this will become your favorite dish—trust me!

1½ to 2 pounds calf's liver, cut into thick strips
1 cup whole milk
2 medium onions, peeled and thinly sliced
½ cup extra-virgin olive oil
¼ cup unsalted butter
½ cup all-purpose flour
3 large egg whites
1 cup fine bread crumbs
1 pound noodles
Juice of 3 lemons
1 tablespoon chopped lemon zest
2 tablespoons sugar
¼ teaspoon white pepper
½ cup chopped Italian parsley

SERVES 4 TO 6

Soak the liver in the milk for several minutes, turning over once.

In a large skillet, sauté the onions in the olive oil and butter. Remove the onions when translucent and set aside. Coat the liver in the flour, dip in the egg whites, and press into the bread crumbs to coat.

Meanwhile, cook the pasta (see page xiii).

Add the liver to the skillet, and brown on both sides, 6 to 8 minutes per side. Return the onions to the skillet.

In a large bowl, combine the noodles, liver, and onions. Using the same skillet, heat the lemon juice, lemon zest, sugar, and pepper. Pour over the noodles, garnish with parsley, and serve.

Mississippi Pasta with Red Beans

So you're thinking, isn't it supposed to be red beans and rice? Well, traditionally yes—however, taste it this way.

1 pound smoked beef or turkey sausage, thinly sliced
1 tablespoon extra-virgin olive oil
1 bunch scallions, chopped
1 clove garlic, minced
1 tablespoon unsalted butter
1 pound dried red beans, presoaked and drained
4 cups chicken stock
1 cup water
1 bay leaf
1 teaspoon hot pepper sauce
Salt to taste (optional)
Freshly ground black pepper to taste
1 pound cavatelli

SERVES 4 TO 6

In a large skillet, sauté the sausage in 1 tablespoon of the olive oil. When the sausage is browned, remove with slotted spoon and discard any rendered fat. Add the scallions and garlic to skillet and sauté briskly in the tablespoon of butter and when scallions are translucent, add the soaked beans, chicken stock, water, bay leaf, hot pepper sauce, salt, and black pepper, and return the sausage to the skillet. Simmer, covered, for about 1½ hours, or until the beans are very soft.

Remove 2 cups of the bean mixture and purée. Return to the pan and cook an additional 30 minutes.

Cook the pasta (see page xiii). Toss with the beans and serve.

Pasta with Swedish Meatballs

We have all eaten Swedish meatballs at a million parties. Now it's time for them to get married with pasta. The sauce calls for using GravyMaster, a commercial seasoning and browning sauce.

THE MEATBALLS

3 slices white bread, chopped
1 small onion, grated
1 tablespoon capers, chopped
¼ teaspoon ground nutmeg
¼ teaspoon white pepper
Salt to taste (optional)
½ cup half-and-half
2 pounds combined ground beef, pork, and veal
1 pound noodles
½ cup chopped Italian parsley

SERVES 4 TO 6

Preheat the oven to 350°F.

Combine the bread, onion, capers, nutmeg, pepper, salt, and cream, and let stand for about 12 minutes.

Mix the bread mixture into the meat mixture and shape into 1¼-inch to 1½-inch meatballs. Put on an ungreased cookie sheet and bake at 350°F for at least 40 minutes, or until cooked.

THE SAUCE

2 tablespoons unsalted butter
2 tablespoons all-purpose flour
2 cups beef stock
1 teaspoon GravyMaster
Salt to taste (optional)
Freshly ground black pepper to taste

Melt the butter in a small saucepan. Add the flour, and continuing to stir, cook until the mixture becomes a tan roux. Add the beef stock, the GravyMaster, salt, and pepper.

Simmer for 15 minutes and add the meatballs; cook until heated through.

THE NOODLES

Cook the pasta (see page xiii). In a large bowl, combine the pasta with the meatballs and gravy. Garnish with parsley and serve.

Noodles with Goulash

2 tablespoons unsalted butter
1 tablespoon extra-virgin olive oil
2 medium onions, chopped
1 clove garlic, minced
1 pound veal for stewing, cut into 1-inch cubes
1 pound lean pork, cut into 1-inch cubes
One 28-ounce can Italian plum tomatoes, undrained
½ teaspoon dried marjoram
2½ teaspoons sweet paprika
1½ teaspoons caraway seeds
1 bay leaf
Freshly ground black pepper to taste
Salt to taste (optional)
1 pound sauerkraut, rinsed and squeezed dry
1 pound wide egg noodles
1½ cups low-fat sour cream

SERVES 4 TO 6

In a large skillet, sauté the onions and garlic in the butter and oil. Add the meat and brown on all sides. Defat if necessary. Reduce the heat and add the tomatoes, breaking them apart in the skillet with a spoon. Add the marjoram, paprika, caraway seeds, bay leaf, pepper, salt, and sauerkraut, cover the skillet, and simmer about 1 hour.

Cook the pasta (see page xiii). Immediately before serving, remove the bay leaf, stir the sour cream into the meat mixture, and adjust the seasonings. Serve over the noodles.

❧ Rigatoni with Okra

1 pound rigatoni
2 cups sliced fresh okra, or one 10-ounce package, frozen
1 cup chopped lean ham
1 medium onion, chopped
¼ cup extra-virgin olive oil
⅛ teaspoon cayenne pepper
¼ cup cherry peppers
Salt to taste (optional)
1 tablespoon tomato paste
½ cup water

SERVES 4 TO 6

Cook the pasta (see page xiii).

In a large skillet, sauté the okra, ham, and onion in the olive oil. (If the okra is frozen, sauté it alone until thawed.) Add the cayenne pepper, cherry peppers, and salt. Mix the tomato paste with the water, add to the skillet, and cover, cooking for about 5 minutes. Serve over individual servings of pasta.

Spaghetti and Meatballs

Not so long ago, Regis Philbin and I got into a discussion about trendy New York Italian restaurants and how he couldn't find spaghetti and meatballs on the menu . . . Well, Reeg–this one's for you!

THE MEATBALLS
½ *pound lean ground beef*
½ *pound lean ground pork*
½ *teaspoon dried oregano*
2 *large eggs or 4 large egg whites, beaten*
2 *tablespoons grated Parmesan cheese*
¾ *cup fine bread crumbs*
Freshly ground black pepper to taste
½ *cup chopped Italian parsley*
Salt to taste (optional)
2 *tablespoons extra-virgin olive oil*

SERVES 4 TO 6

Mix the meat with all the other ingredients, except the olive oil. Form the mixture into 8 meatballs.

In a large skillet, heat the oil over medium heat and with a cover on, cook the meatballs for 20 minutes, until the internal temperature is 180°F, turning occasionally.

Alternatively, the meatballs can be baked in the oven. Preheat the oven to 400°F and bake the meatballs for 20 minutes. Reduce the oven temperature to 375°F and bake for an additional 30 to 40 minutes, or until the internal temperature of the meatballs is 180°F.

THE SAUCE

1 small onion, chopped
2 cloves garlic, minced
¼ cup extra-virgin olive oil
One 35-ounce can Italian plum tomatoes with their juice
3 ounces tomato paste
3 ounces water
1 teaspoon salt
2 pinches dried basil
1 pinch dried thyme
Freshly ground black pepper to taste
Grated Parmesan cheese

THE PASTA

1 pound spaghetti

To make the sauce, sauté the onion and garlic in the olive oil for about 5 minutes. Chop the tomatoes coarsely, and add, with the juices, to the skillet. Add the tomato paste, water, salt, basil, thyme, and pepper and simmer, covered, for 30 minutes.

Add the meatballs to the sauce and cook, covered, an additional 30 minutes. Remove the cover, stir, and cook another 20 to 25 minutes.

While the sauce is simmering, cook the pasta (see page xiii). When ready, serve the sauce and meatballs over the pasta and sprinkle with cheese.

Pasta with Fried Peppers

For this dish, try to find Italian frying peppers. They are long, narrow, and perfect with pasta.

3 tablespoons extra-virgin olive oil
3 cloves garlic
1 medium carrot, julienne
1 medium onion, chopped
6 Italian frying peppers, cut into strips
¼ pound Italian salami, sliced thin, cut into strips ¼-inch wide
1 tablespoon balsamic vinegar
¼ teaspoon dried oregano
Freshly ground black pepper to taste
Salt to taste (optional)
1 pound rigatoni
½ cup pasta water
¼ cup grated Parmesan cheese

SERVES 4 TO 6

In a medium skillet, heat the oil and sauté the garlic, carrot, and onion; discard the garlic when it turns golden and add the peppers, salami, vinegar, oregano, pepper, and salt. Cover and sauté for another 15 minutes.

Meanwhile, cook the pasta (see page xiii). Reserve ½ cup water when draining and add to the skillet. In a large bowl, combine the pasta, pepper mixture, and cheese. Toss well and serve.

Meat-filled Cannelloni

12 large cannelloni (tubes)
1 tablespoon extra-virgin olive oil
1 tablespoon unsalted butter
1 small onion, chopped
One 1/2-inch slice prosciutto or ham, chopped
1 cup chicken stock
1 large chicken breast (1 1/2 pounds), skinless and boned
1/2 cup chopped mushrooms
1/2 cup white wine
2 large egg whites
1/4 teaspoon ground nutmeg
1/4 teaspoon white pepper
Salt to taste (optional)
1/4 cup grated Parmesan cheese
1 tablespoon chopped Italian parsley
2 tablespoons bread crumbs
1 quart marinara sauce (page 178)

12 CANNELLONI

Cook the pasta (see page xiii). Drain, rinse in cold water, and drain again.

In a large skillet heat the oil and butter and briefly sauté the onion until it is soft. Add the prosciutto, chicken stock, chicken, mushrooms, and wine. Cover and simmer for 12 to 15 minutes, until the chicken is cooked and the liquid is reduced.

Preheat the oven to 375°F. Transfer the skillet mixture to a food processor and process into a fine paste. Transfer to a bowl, add the egg whites, nutmeg, pepper, salt, Parmesan cheese, parsley, and bread crumbs, and mix well.

Oil a baking dish and spoon some of the sauce on the bottom. Fill the pasta tubes with the meat and vegetable mixture and ladle sauce on top of each tube. Bake, uncovered, for about 20 minutes. Serve.

Orzo with Veal Shanks

6 large veal shanks, 3 inches thick by 4 to 4½ inches wide (if small,
    allow 2 per person)
½ cup all-purpose flour
2 tablespoons unsalted butter
2 tablespoons extra-virgin olive oil
1 cup dry white wine
2 cups beef stock
2 cups canned Italian plum tomatoes, drained and slightly crushed
⅛ teaspoon dried sage
Freshly ground black pepper to taste
Salt to taste (optional)
8 ounces orzo
Juice of 1 lemon
1 tablespoon grated lemon zest
Italian parsley sprigs, for garnish

SERVES 6

Dredge the veal shanks in the flour. In a large skillet, heat the butter
with the oil and put all the shanks in one layer. Brown the shanks on all
sides over medium-high heat.

Reduce the heat to low and add ¼ cup wine and ¼ cup stock. Cover
and cook at a slow simmer for 40 minutes.

Remove the shanks and defat the pan juices. Add the tomatoes, the
remaining stock, sage, pepper, and salt, and combine.

Return the shanks to the skillet and add the remaining wine. Cover
and continue to cook for 1¾ to 2 hours, making sure that the contents do
not boil but simmer very slowly.

Cook the pasta (see page xiii), but add the juice of one lemon to the
water.

The meat should be very tender, so use tongs to remove the shanks to
a warm platter when done. Sprinkle some lemon zest on each shank. Raise

the heat, add the chopped parsley, and reduce the sauce by one half. Place each shank on an individual serving plate and encircle it with orzo. Spoon on the sauce, crisscrossing over the meat. Garnish with parsley sprigs and serve.

East Eighty-sixth Street Pasta

East Eighty-sixth Street in Manhattan was the site of New York's Germantown—and the site of the Cooking with Love school. This pasta dish is reminiscent of the best of German cooking.

1 tablespoon extra-virgin olive oil
1½ pounds veal for stewing, cut into 1-inch cubes
2 tablespoons unsalted butter
2 cloves garlic
½ cup sliced almonds
1 cup beef stock
1 pound broad noodles
1⅛ teaspoons paprika
2 teaspoons poppy seeds
1 cup sour cream
Salt to taste (optional)

SERVES 4 TO 6

In a large skillet, heat the oil and cook the meat until it is browned on all sides. Remove, set aside and defat the skillet. Add the butter, garlic, and almonds and cook until golden and then discard the garlic. Return the meat to the skillet, and add the stock. Cover and simmer for 1½ hours.

Meanwhile, cook the pasta (see page xiii).

Mix the paprika and poppy seeds with the sour cream and add the mixture to the skillet. Mix thoroughly and add the salt. Heat through and serve over the noodles.

Korean Pasta

1 large dried mushroom
¾ pound fettuccine
½ pound pork, cut into strips
½ bunch scallions, sliced
2 tablespoons sesame oil
½ pound large shrimp, shelled, deveined, and sliced
One 8-ounce can baby corn
½ tablespoon cornstarch
2 tablespoon light soy sauce
2 tablespoons sherry
2 egg whites
Salt to taste (optional)

SERVES 4 TO 6

Soak the mushroom in warm water until soft, then slice.

Cook the pasta (see page xiii).

Meanwhile, in a large skillet or wok, stir the pork, mushroom, and scallions in the sesame oil. When the pork is cooked, add the shrimp and corn.

Mix the cornstarch with the soy sauce and sherry and add slowly to the skillet. Add the egg whites and salt. Toss with the pasta.

Japanese Curly Noodles
with Beef Teriyaki

Across from the tour bus station in a small Japanese neighborhood was this little local noodle shop where all the locals were lunching. Needless to say, even though no English was spoken, I tasted many delicious dishes before getting on the bus—with a big smile! The Japanese curly noodles, or ramen, are readily available in five-ounce packages.

15 ounces Japanese curly noodles
¾ pound beef, cut into 3- × 1-inch strips
2 tablespoons extra-virgin olive oil
1 bunch scallions, sliced
½ cup sliced cashew nuts
1 teaspoon ground ginger
3 tablespoons light soy sauce
¼ cup teriyaki sauce
4 ounces button mushrooms
¼ cup pasta water
Salt to taste (optional)

SERVES 4 TO 6

Cook the noodles as directed on the package. Reserve ¼ cup of pasta water when draining.

In a large skillet, sauté the beef in the olive oil for about 10 minutes. Add the scallions, cashew nuts, ginger, soy sauce, teriyaki sauce, and mushrooms, and stir-fry. Stir in the cooked noodles, pasta water, and salt. Toss and serve.

Chinese-style Pasta

On a Chinese menu you will see various lo mein dishes. "Mein" means noodles made from wheat, whereas "fun," as in chow fun, is the designation for noodles made from rice. This dish works equally well with either.

Three 4-ounce turkey cutlets
½ cup all-purpose flour
2 tablespoons extra-virgin olive oil
2 tablespoons cornstarch
3 tablespoons water
1 teaspoon sugar
2 tablespoons light soy sauce
1 pound vermicelli
1 medium carrot, cut into matchsticks
1 clove garlic, chopped
1 cup chicken stock
2 cups fresh bean sprouts

SERVES 4 TO 6

Dust the turkey with flour. In a medium skillet, sauté the turkey in olive oil. Remove the turkey when cooked. Cut into strips, and set aside. In a small jar, shake together the cornstarch, water, sugar, and soy sauce. Meanwhile, cook the pasta (see page xiii).

Add the carrot and garlic to the skillet and sauté for 1 to 2 minutes. Add the chicken stock, then add the cornstarch mixture and cook until the mixture thickens. Add the bean sprouts and return the turkey to the skillet and heat through. In a large bowl, combine the pasta and turkey mixture and toss well. Serve.

🌿 Pork Lo Mein

Many take-out Chinese restaurants let their lo mein get soggy. See what a difference your freshly cooked or fresh noodles will make in this dish.

2 large dried shiitake mushrooms
½ pound dried Oriental noodles
1 tablespoon sesame oil
3 tablespoons vegetable oil
1¼ to 1½ pounds lean pork loin, cut into thin strips
½ cup bamboo shoots, cut into thin strips
3 scallions, sliced
2 cups fresh bean sprouts, soaked in water and drained
3 tablespoons sherry
1 tablespoon oyster sauce
2 tablespoons soy sauce

SERVES 4 TO 6

Soak the mushrooms in warm water 30 minutes before you start cooking. Squeeze out the water from the mushrooms. Cut the mushrooms into thin strips.

Cook the noodles, drain, rinse in cold water, drain again, and toss with the sesame oil. Set aside.

Heat the vegetable oil in a wok or skillet. Stir-fry the pork for about 8 minutes until browned, and add the mushrooms. Stir-fry for 1 minute more. Add the bamboo shoots, scallions, bean sprouts, sherry, and oyster sauce. Mix and stir-fry for 3 minutes more.

Add the cooked noodles to the wok and sprinkle with soy sauce. Mix thoroughly to combine with other ingredients. Stir-fry an additional 4 minutes. The pork must be completely cooked. Serve.

❧ Chinese Egg Foo Yung

Here's a twist on this old Chinese dish! Spinach fettuccine gives it a fresh, new taste.

½ *pound spinach fettuccine, broken into small pieces*
6 *large eggs*
Pinch of salt
Freshly ground black pepper to taste
2 *cups bean sprouts, preferably fresh*
Extra-virgin olive oil
½ *cup chopped scallions*
1 *cup cooked chopped ham, turkey, or chicken (optional)*
Soy sauce
Hot pepper sauce

SERVES 4

❧

Cook the pasta (see page xiii).

In a large bowl, beat the eggs with the salt and pepper, and add the sprouts. In a lightly oiled 6-inch skillet, sauté the scallions until they are translucent, about 6 minutes. Add the scallions to the egg mixture. Add your choice of meat. Brush more oil on the skillet (unless it is a nonstick pan) and when it is hot, add one quarter of the egg mixture, then add one quarter of the cooked pasta. Brown on one side, flip over, and brown on the other side. Repeat for the remaining servings. Serve with soy sauce and hot pepper sauce on the side.

Father's Day Loaf Pasta

This is the one dish when you're allowed to have the ketchup bottle on the table.

12 ounces elbows
1 large carrot
2 egg yolks
½ cup barbecue sauce
1 teaspoon Worcestershire sauce
½ teaspoon white pepper
½ teaspoon garlic powder
¼ teaspoon dried thyme
½ teaspoon hot pepper sauce
Salt to taste (optional)
1 medium onion, chopped
½ cup chopped Italian parsley
1¼ to ½12 pounds corned beef brisket, cooked and shredded
3 egg whites

SERVES 4 TO 6

Preheat the oven to 350°F. Grease a loaf pan.

Cook the pasta (see page xiii). Reserve the pasta water and add the whole carrot to the water; cook until al dente. Rinse and drain well.

In a medium bowl, beat the egg yolks. Add the barbecue sauce, Worcestershire sauce, pepper, garlic powder, thyme, hot pepper sauce, salt, onion, parsley, and brisket, and mix well. Add the elbows. Beat the egg whites until stiff and fold into mixture.

Pour half of the mixture into the loaf pan; lay the carrot in the center and spoon the remaining mixture over top.

Bake at 350°F for 50 to 60 minutes or until 160°F on an instant-read thermometer. Spoon or invert on a serving dish and slice to serve.

✤ Uncle Tony's Pasta

Uncle Tony would make this pasta on a moment's notice. The ingredients were always in the fridge and on the shelves.

1 pound noodles
1 small onion, peeled and grated
2 tablespoons extra-virgin olive oil
2 tablespoons unsalted butter
1 teaspoon paprika
¼ cup whole milk
Salt to taste (optional)
Freshly ground black pepper to taste
3 tablespoons poppy seeds
6 slices bacon, cooked very well and crumbled

SERVES 4 TO 6

✤

Cook the pasta (see page xiii).

Meanwhile, in a medium skillet, sauté the onion with the olive oil and butter. Add the paprika, milk, salt, and pepper.

In a large bowl, combine the noodles with the sauce; add the poppy seeds and bacon and toss well. Serve.

St. Patrick's Day Pasta

As a little boy, I used to march in the New York City St. Patrick's Day parade with my bugle, and later my trumpet. I wish I had had a big bowl of this pasta before each parade!!

1 pound medium-wide noodles
3 tablespoons extra-virgin olive oil
1 tablespoon unsalted butter
1 medium onion, peeled and chopped
½ small green pepper, seeded and chopped
1 large cooked potato, cold, diced
1 pound cooked lean corned beef, coarsely chopped
Freshly ground black pepper to taste
2 teaspoons Worcestershire sauce
2 dashes hot pepper sauce
½ cup chopped parsley

SERVES 4 TO 6

Cook the pasta (see page xiii).

In a large skillet, sauté the onion, green pepper, and potato in the olive oil and butter. Add the corned beef, and when crisp, add the pepper, Worcestershire sauce, hot sauce, and chopped parsley. Toss with the noodles and serve.

Pasta with Seafood

The sea and the earth provide sustenance that has a rich combination of flavors and nutrition.

My mom loves soft-shell crabs and I remember her making them for herself when I was young. My brother, Dad, and I would not eat them and she used to say, *"You don't know what you're missing."* How many times have we all heard that before? Well, Mom, here is my *Maryland Pasta*, full of your soft-shell crabs combined with white wine, clam juice, and suffused with fennel seeds, sweet paprika, lemon juice, and tossed with linguine.

When fresh salmon is nestled in a bath of heavily brandied cream tossed with fettuccine, your guests and family will yell bravo!

The simple yet delicious anchovy sauce, when tossed with linguine or my fettuccine mixed with shrimp and coconut, will further prove that if you are stranded on an island, just make sure you brought pasta.

❧ Pasta with Trout

1 large red onion, chopped
3 tablespoons extra-virgin olive oil
Juice of ½ lemon
½ cup chopped Italian parsley
Freshly ground black pepper to taste
Salt to taste (optional)
1 pound linguine
½ cup all-purpose flour
½ cup bread crumbs
½ tablespoon fennel seeds
½ teaspoon paprika
¼ teaspoon white pepper
6 trout fillets
1 tablespoon unsalted butter
½ cup pasta water

SERVES 4 TO 6

In a large skillet, sauté the onion in 1 tablespoon of the olive oil. Add the lemon juice, parsley, pepper, and salt. When the onion is translucent, remove and set aside.

Cook the pasta (see page xiii). Reserve ½ cup pasta water when draining.

Mix the flour with the bread crumbs, fennel seeds, paprika, and pepper. Dredge the trout in the flour mixture and add the remaining olive oil and butter to the skillet. Sauté the trout on each side until golden, about 2 minutes per side, adding additional butter and oil if needed.

In the meantime, toss the pasta with the onion mixture and the pasta water, and distribute on a serving plate. Put a fillet on top of each plate and serve.

Alaskan Seafood Pasta

The pristine waters of Alaska give us the finest halibut, and here I give you one of the finest pasta recipes for the fish that can't be tuna!

½ pound small shells
4 tablespoons extra-virgin olive oil
12 medium shrimp, peeled and deveined
½ pound bay or sea scallops (sea scallops should be halved)
¾ pound halibut fillet, cut into 3-inch-long pieces
1 small head broccoli
2 red or yellow bell peppers
1 carrot
3 large mushrooms
1 bay leaf
Pinch of marjoram
¼ teaspoon oregano
½ cup dry white wine
Juice of ½ lemon
Freshly ground black pepper to taste
Salt to taste (optional)
Dash of crushed red pepper, if desired

SERVES 4 TO 6

Cook the pasta (see page xiii).

Brush the oil on one side of a large piece of heavy-duty extra-wide aluminum foil. Put the seafood and fish in the center of that half. (The other half will cover the food.)

Wash the broccoli and bell peppers, peel the carrot, and wipe off the mushrooms. Do not shake off any excess water. Cut the vegetables into bite-size pieces and place them on top of the seafood. Scatter the cooked pasta over everything.

Turn up the edges of the foil so that the liquid will not escape, and sprinkle the food with the bay leaf, marjoram, oregano, wine, lemon juice, and pepper. Add salt and crushed red pepper, if desired. Bring the other half of the foil down over the food and carefully fold the two edges together all the way around to seal the packet.

To grill, put the packet on the grill and cook for 20 to 25 minutes. Check to see if the fish is done by carefully opening one side of the foil packet and test for doneness to your liking. If your grill has a lid, you can open the top of the foil packet after the first 15 minutes of cooking and finish cooking with the grill hood closed. When cooked in this manner, the fish will have a smoky taste. For gas or electric grills, set the heat medium-low.

Alternatively, cook the packets in a preheated oven, and bake for 20 to 25 minutes at 350°F, or until cooked. Serve when hot.

Caribbean Seafood Pasta

Over the years I developed this recipe for a liquor company. Millions of recipes were sent out and this one has been enjoyed by many!

8 ounces medium shells
1/3 cup extra-virgin olive oil
1 pound firm-flesh fish fillets, such as cod, scrod, grouper, or snapper, cut
    into large chunks
1/2 pound fresh mushrooms, thinly sliced (2 cups)
1 red bell pepper, cut into strips (1 cup)
1/2 cup thickly sliced celery
1/2 cup sliced scallions
1 clove garlic, minced
One 8-ounce can water chestnuts, drained and sliced
1/2 cup coconut rum liqueur
2 tablespoons soy sauce
1 tablespoon cornstarch

SERVES 4 TO 6

Cook the pasta (see page xiii).

In a large skillet, heat the oil and cook the fish on all sides until it is flaky, about 3 minutes. Remove the fish and set aside. In the same skillet, stir-fry the mushrooms, bell pepper, celery, scallions, garlic, and water chestnuts about 3 minutes, until the vegetables are crisp but tender. In a small bowl, mix the coconut rum liqueur, soy sauce, and cornstarch, add to the skillet, and stir until the mixture thickens. Return the fish to the skillet and mix gently into the vegetables. Cook just long enough to heat the fish. Drain the pasta well and mix together. Serve.

Pasta and Oysters

The "romantic" claim for oysters can now have the addition of "pasta energy." E-mail me the results at: lovechef@www.lovechef.com.

1 pound fusilli
2 cloves garlic
1 small onion, chopped
1 stalk celery, sliced
½ carrot, thinly sliced
¼ cup extra-virgin olive oil
1 teaspoon drained capers
Juice of 1 lemon
¼ cup chopped Italian parsley
Freshly ground black pepper to taste
Salt to taste (optional)
Dash hot pepper sauce
24 oysters, cleaned and shucked, or 24 mussels, cleaned and shucked
1 pound medium shrimp, peeled and deveined

SERVES 4 TO 6

Cook the pasta (see page xiii).

In a large skillet, sauté garlic, onion, celery, and carrot in the olive oil. When the garlic turns golden, remove and discard. Add the capers, lemon juice, parsley, pepper, salt, and hot pepper sauce. Add the oysters and shrimp and sauté for about 5 minutes. Toss with the pasta and serve.

❧ Caviar Pasta

Of course, in this recipe I am using the pasteurized caviar from a jar, which can be bought in a supermarket. These are not the eggs (caviar) of sturgeon, which are very costly and perishable.

1 pound linguine
1 bunch scallions, chopped
1 tablespoon extra-virgin olive oil
2 cups low-fat sour cream
One 4-ounce jar black lumpfish caviar
¼ teaspoon white pepper

SERVES 4 TO 6

❧

Cook the pasta (see page xiii).

Meanwhile, in a medium skillet, briefly sauté the scallions, just long enough to lose rawness, in the olive oil. Add the sour cream, caviar, and pepper. Reduce the heat to low, and do not let the mixture boil. When heated through, toss the mixture with pasta and serve.

✺ Norwegian Pasta with Codfish

Codfish is a hearty, flaky white-meat fish—a great value for family meals.

1 pound shells
1½ pounds codfish fillets
2 egg yolks (reserve whites)
1½ cups milk
2 tablespoons unsalted butter, melted
1 tablespoon capers
1 cup bread crumbs
½ teaspoon dried dill
¼ teaspoon white pepper
Salt to taste (optional)
3 egg whites

SERVES 4 TO 6

❧

Preheat the oven to 350°F. Grease a 9- × 13- × 2-inch baking dish. Cook the pasta (see page xiii).

Meanwhile, in a large saucepan over medium-low heat poach the fillets, 8 to 10 minutes.

In a medium bowl, beat the egg yolks, and add the milk, butter, capers, bread crumbs, dill, pepper, and salt. Flake the cooked fish fillets and add to the bowl, taking care to remove any skin or bones. Add the pasta to the fish mixture and mix thoroughly.

In a separate bowl, beat the egg whites until stiff and fold into the fish mixture. Pour the mixture into the baking dish, cover, and bake at 350°F for 40 to 45 minutes. Serve.

Pasta with White Clam Sauce

The small amount of work needed to create this masterpiece is well worth the results when you taste it!

3 pounds cherrystone clams (about 36 clams)
1 pound linguine or vermicelli
1 clove garlic, crushed
½ cup extra-virgin olive oil
3 tablespoons unsalted butter
1 cup bottled clam juice
¾ cup white wine
½ teaspoon white pepper
Juice of ½ lemon
¼ cup chopped Italian parsley
Salt to taste (optional)

SERVES 4 TO 6

Wash the clams thoroughly and place them in a large saucepan with 1 cup water, cover, and steam until they open; discard any that don't open. Remove the clams with a slotted spoon, strain the liquid, and set aside. Remove the clams from their shells, discarding the brown sac in each clam. Chop the flesh and set aside.

Cook the pasta (see page xiii).

Meanwhile, in a medium skillet, sauté the garlic in the olive oil. Discard when it turns golden. Add the butter, reserved clam juice, bottled clam juice, white wine, and pepper. Simmer for 5 to 8 minutes, then add the clams, lemon juice, parsley, and salt and cook an additional 3 minutes. Toss with the pasta and serve.

PASTA WITH RED CLAM SAUCE

2 cups canned tomatoes, crushed

Add the tomatoes to the skillet after sautéing the garlic with the butter, reserved clam juice, bottled clam juice, white wine, and pepper. Simmer for 12 to 15 minutes. Continue to follow the directions for Pasta with White Clam Sauce.

Pasta with Washington Salmon

*Here, the famous onion from Walla Walla, hailed as the sweetest in all the
land, along with salmon, makes an excellent candlelight dinner in no time.*

2 large Walla Walla onions, chopped
4 tablespoons extra-virgin olive oil
One 14¾-ounce can salmon
1 tablespoon capers
½ teaspoon white pepper
Salt to taste (optional)
¼ teaspoon crushed red pepper
1 cup bottled clam juice
1 pound fusilli
½ cup chopped Italian parsley

SERVES 4 TO 6

In a large skillet, sauté the onions in olive oil until brown. Clean the
salmon of any remaining bone or skin and add to the skillet with the
capers, white pepper, salt, crushed red pepper, and clam juice. Break apart
the salmon and mix.

Cook the pasta (see page xiii). Spoon the mixture over the pasta, garnish with the parsley, and serve.

Pasta with Crabmeat

1 small onion, chopped
2 cloves garlic, chopped
¼ cup extra-virgin olive oil
One 35-ounce can Italian plum tomatoes, undrained
1 cup bottled clam juice
1 teaspoon salt
1 teaspoon lemon juice
2 pinches dried basil
⅛ teaspoon crushed red pepper
¼ teaspoon dried thyme
Freshly ground black pepper to taste
2½ cups crabmeat
1 pound linguine

SERVES 4 TO 6

In a large skillet, sauté the onion and garlic in the oil for about 5 minutes. Chop the tomatoes coarsely and add with their juices to the skillet. Add the clam juice, salt, lemon juice, basil, crushed red pepper, thyme, and pepper. Cook, covered, for 10 minutes; stir and cook uncovered for another 15 minutes. Add the crabmeat and cook another 10 minutes.

Meanwhile, cook the pasta (see page xiii). When ready, serve the sauce over the pasta.

Replace the crabmeat with lobster meat.

Maryland Pasta with Soft-shell Crabs

Great crabs from this state make a terrific pasta.

1 pound linguine
6 medium soft-shell crabs, cleaned
4 tablespoons extra-virgin olive oil
2 tablespoons unsalted butter
2 cloves garlic
1 teaspoon fennel seeds
1 teaspoon sweet paprika
Juice of ½ lemon
1 cup dry white wine
1 cup bottled clam juice
Salt to taste (optional)
Freshly ground black pepper to taste
½ cup chopped Italian parsley

SERVES 4 TO 6

Cook the pasta (see page xiii).

In a large skillet, sauté the crabs in the olive oil and butter with the garlic cloves. Cook for 3 minutes on each side, then remove the crabs and keep warm. Add the fennel seeds, paprika, and lemon juice and cook briefly. Add the wine, clam juice, salt, and pepper and cook for about 12 minutes. Add the parsley.

Toss with the pasta and add a crab to each serving.

Hawaiian Pasta with Pineapple and Shrimp

This is a summer pasta salad that goes well with a barbecue, especially one serving ribs and pork.

¾ pound radiators
8 ounces tiny shrimp
½ cup mayonnaise
½ cup sour cream
One 8-ounce can Hawaiian pineapple chunks, drained
¼ cup sliced almonds
¼ teaspoon white pepper
Salt to taste (optional)

SERVES 4 TO 6

Cook the pasta (see page xiii).

Cook the shrimp and drain well. In a large bowl, add the mayonnaise, sour cream, pineapple chunks, almonds, white pepper, and salt.

Drain the pasta, rinse under cold water, and shake dry. Refrigerate until chilled or freeze for a few minutes to speed up the process. Combine the mixture with the chilled pasta and adjust the seasonings to taste. Serve.

Pasta and Bacalao

Bacalao is codfish that is cleaned, dried, and preserved with salt. Recently I frequented a restaurant in Madrid, Spain, where the chef made me a Basque version of bacalao. I ate the whole portion for two. This from a little boy growing up who couldn't stand to be in the house when my mom would fix this on Christmas Eve.

1½ pounds bacalao (dried, salted cod)
1 cup chopped celery leaves
2 large onions, chopped
1 pound ripe plum tomatoes, chopped
½ teaspoon dried oregano
1 teaspoon capers, rinsed
2 mild chilies, sliced
½ cup extra-virgin olive oil
1 pound penne

SERVES 4 TO 6

Soak the bacalao in water for 4 to 6 hours; then drain. Boil in water to cover with celery leaves for 15 to 20 minutes.

Drain and rinse, discarding the skin and bones. Shred the flesh.

Meanwhile, in a large skillet, sauté the onions, tomatoes, oregano, capers, and chilies in olive oil until the onions are translucent.

Cook the pasta (see page xiii).

Add the fish to the skillet, heat through, and spoon over the pasta.

Pasta with Sardines

2 cloves garlic
4 tablespoons extra-virgin olive oil
One 8-ounce can sardines
One 35-ounce can crushed tomatoes
1 dozen pitted black olives, sliced
1 tablespoon capers
¼ teaspoon crushed red pepper
Freshly ground black pepper to taste
½ cup chopped Italian parsley
1 pound fusilli

SERVES 4 TO 6

In a medium skillet, sauté the garlic in the oil and discard when it turns golden. Add the sardines and simmer, breaking up the sardines with a spoon. Add the tomatoes, olives, capers, crushed red pepper, pepper, and parsley. Cook for 18 minutes.

Cook the pasta (see page xiii). Toss with the sauce and serve.

Pasta with Conch

You've tasted conch fritters, but now enjoy this as a dressing over pasta.

1 pound conch meat (fresh or canned), sliced
1 pound linguine or vermicelli
2 cloves garlic, crushed
¼ cup extra-virgin olive oil
2 tablespoons unsalted butter
1 cup bottled clam juice
½ cup dry white wine
½ teaspoon white pepper
1 teaspoon fresh lemon juice
½ cup chopped Italian parsley
Salt to taste (optional)

SERVES 4 TO 6

Wash the conch meat thoroughly, and put it in a large saucepan with 1 cup water, cover, and steam until tender. Remove the conch with a slotted spoon, then strain the pan juices, and set aside. Chop the flesh and set aside.

Cool the pasta (see page xiii).

Meanwhile, in a medium skillet, sauté the garlic in the olive oil, discarding it when it turns golden. Add the butter, reserved conch juice, bottled clam juice, white wine, and pepper. Simmer for 5 to 8 minutes, and add the conch, lemon juice, parsley, and salt and cook an additional 3 minutes. Toss with the pasta and serve.

Pasta with Mussels

½ cup fish stock or water
1 cup dry white wine
1 tablespoon fresh lemon juice
4 dozen mussels, washed and scrubbed
1 pound linguine
1 clove garlic, crushed
¼ cup extra-virgin olive oil
1½ cups canned plum tomatoes, undrained, chopped
½ teaspoon dried thyme
¼ teaspoon dried basil
¼ teaspoon crushed red pepper
Freshly ground black pepper to taste
Salt to taste (optional)
2 tablespoons chopped Italian parsley

SERVES 4 TO 6

Put the stock, wine, and lemon juice in a stockpot and bring to a boil. Add the mussels, cover, and simmer for about 5 minutes until they open.

Cook the pasta (see page xiii).

Remove the mussels, strain the liquid through a cheesecloth, and discard any unopened mussels.

In a large skillet, sauté the garlic in the olive oil until the garlic is golden and then discard. Add the tomatoes, thyme, basil, red pepper, black pepper, and salt and simmer for about 6 minutes. Add the strained liquid and cook another 4 minutes. Add the mussels to the skillet and cook another 2 minutes, or until they are thoroughly heated. Mix with the pasta, add the parsley, and serve.

Shrimp and Pasta Salad for the Beach

If there is a particular spice that you like or dislike, adjust the recipe accordingly!

¾ pound small shells
¼ cup extra-virgin olive oil
¾ cup low-fat mayonnaise
½ pound baby shrimp, cooked
1 pound sea legs, cut into small pieces
1 teaspoon capers, drained
1 stalk celery, sliced
Juice of 1 lemon
¼ teaspoon ground turmeric
½ cup ground fresh cilantro
Freshly ground black pepper to taste
Salt to taste (optional)

SERVES 4 TO 6

Cook the pasta (see page xiii). Drain well and refrigerate until cool.

In a large bowl, combine the olive oil and mayonnaise, and add the shrimp, sea legs, capers, celery, lemon juice, turmeric, cilantro, pepper, and salt. Mix well and serve.

Grandpa's Shrimp, Scallop, and Cod with Linguine

When you have a barbecue going and hungry people around, bring out this cooked pasta and the rest is easy.

¼ cup extra-virgin olive oil
8 medium shrimp, peeled and deveined
½ pound bay scallops
½ pound cod fillet, cut into small pieces
1 carrot, thinly sliced
½ head broccoli, cut into florets
½ head cauliflower, cut into florets
2 bay leaves
¼ teaspoon dried oregano leaves
Pinch dried marjoram leaves
Pinch crushed red pepper
Salt to taste (optional)
Freshly ground black pepper to taste
½ cup white wine
Juice of ½ lemon
1 pound linguine

SERVES 6

Brush the oil on one side of a large piece of heavy-duty extra-wide aluminum foil. Place all the seafood in the center of that half. (The other half will cover the food.)

Leave any excess water clinging to the vegetables and place them on top of the seafood. Turn up the edges of the foil so that the liquid will not escape. Sprinkle the vegetables with the remaining olive oil, bay leaf, oregano, marjoram, and red pepper flakes. Season with salt and pepper. Add the wine and lemon juice. Bring the other half of the foil down over the food and carefully fold the two edges together all the way around to seal the packet.

To grill, put the foil packet on the grill and cook for 20 to 25 minutes. Check to see if the fish is done by carefully opening one side of the foil packet. If your grill has a lid, you can open the top of the packet after the first 15 minutes of cooking and finish cooking with the grill hood closed. For a gas or electric grills, set the heat at medium-low.

Alternatively, cook the packet in a preheated 350°F oven for 40 to 50 minutes, or until cooked.

Cook the pasta (see page xiii). Remove the bay leaf from the packet. Toss the cooked pasta with the contents of the foil packet and serve.

Fettuccine with Shrimp and Coconut

Buy plain coconut juice—a different taste from the ordinary. Coconut juice is widely available in most supermarkets, and not to be confused with the sugar-sweetened concentrate.

1 pound fettuccine
1 medium onion, chopped
2 medium green peppers, seeded and chopped
2 tablespoons extra-virgin olive oil
2 medium tomatoes, chopped
1 cup coconut juice (or 11.8-ounce can)
¼ cup fresh cilantro, chopped
¼ teaspoon white pepper
Salt to taste (optional)
1 pound medium shrimp, shelled and deveined

SERVES 4 TO 6

Cook the pasta (see page xiii).

Sauté the onion and green peppers in the olive oil in a medium skillet until soft. Add the tomatoes and coconut juice, cilantro, pepper, salt, and shrimp. Continue cooking until the shrimp are opaque. Toss the pasta with the shrimp and serve.

Pasta with Anchovy Sauce

I am an anchovy lover and, if you are also, this pasta sauce will have you danc-ing in the kitchen.

1 pound linguine
1 medium onion, chopped
3 tablespoons extra-virgin olive oil
2 tablespoons all-purpose flour
1 cup heavy cream
1/8 teaspoon white pepper
Juice of 1/4 lemon
One 2-ounce can anchovy fillets (rinsed)
1/2 cup pasta water
1/2 cup chopped Italian parsley

SERVES 4 TO 6

Cook the pasta (see page xiii). Reserve 1/2 cup of the water when draining.

In a large skillet (large enough to hold pasta), sauté the onions in one tablespoon of olive oil until translucent. Remove and set aside. Add the remaining 2 tablespoons of olive oil and then the flour and cook over low heat to make a roux. When the roux is medium tan, add the cream and reduce by half over medium heat, stirring frequently. Add the pepper and lemon juice, and blend in the anchovies. Return the onions to the skillet and simmer for 2 to 3 minutes.

Add the pasta water and the pasta to the skillet, mix and cook. Add the parsley and toss. Serve.

Linguine with Scallops

1 pound linguine
3 cloves garlic
6 tablespoons extra-virgin olive oil
6 plum tomatoes, diced
2 tablespoons fresh lemon juice
⅛ teaspoon white pepper
2 tablespoons minced Italian parsley
½ cup pasta water
1 pound bay or sea scallops (cut sea scallops into small pieces)

SERVES 4 TO 6

Cook the pasta (see page xiii). Reserve ½ cup water when draining.

In a large skillet, sauté the garlic in the oil until it turns brown, and discard. Add the tomatoes, lemon juice, pepper, and parsley. Add the water. Stir, and then add the scallops, and stir often. Cook until they are opaque, 4 to 5 minutes. Toss the pasta with the scallops and sauce, and serve.

❦ Pasta with Salmon

Several years ago, I received a gift of fresh salmon from Seattle. I remember the day was very stormy, so I cooked up a batch of this while I sipped some brandy, one of the ingredients. My neighbors all ate well that evening.

6 shallots, minced
4 tablespoons unsalted butter
4 tablespoons extra-virgin olive oil
1 pound fresh salmon, cut into 1-inch cubes
1 pound fettuccine
½ cup brandy
1 cup heavy cream
2 cups chopped ripe tomatoes
½ teaspoon white pepper
⅛ teaspoon ground nutmeg
Salt to taste (optional)
½ cup chopped Italian parsley

SERVES 4 TO 6

In a large skillet, sauté the shallots in butter and olive oil until the shallots are soft. Add the salmon and sauté for 2 to 3 minutes.

Meanwhile, cook the pasta (see page xiii).

Add the brandy to the skillet and carefully ignite with a match. When the flame subsides, add the cream and tomatoes, and stir. Cook for about 15 minutes, until the sauce reduces and thickens. Add the pepper, nutmeg, and salt. Toss the pasta with some sauce to coat, and then add the remaining sauce to the pasta. Garnish with parsley and serve.

Sautéed Squid and Pasta

To many, squid or calamari is a rubbery mass that serves as a base for a deep-fried coating and a thick layer of cocktail sauce. But in this recipe, squid takes its rightful place as the centerpiece of an especially flavorful dish—and it is perfect served over a steamy plate of pasta.

3 cloves garlic
3 tablespoons extra-virgin olive oil
1 tablespoon unsalted butter
1 pound cleaned squid, cut into bite-size pieces
1 pound linguine
¾ cup dry white wine
3 tablespoons chopped Italian parsley
Juice of ½ lemon
½ teaspoon crushed red pepper
Freshly ground black pepper to taste
Salt to taste (optional)

SERVES 4 TO 6

In a medium skillet, sauté the garlic in the oil and butter until it turns golden, then discard the garlic. Add the squid and sauté for 3 to 5 minutes.

Cook the pasta as usual (see page xiii).

Remove the squid and add the wine, parsley, lemon juice, red pepper, black pepper, and salt, and reduce the sauce by half. Pour the liquid over the squid and toss with the pasta. Serve.

Pasta with "Saucy" Sauces

This mix of recipes is from the category of "comfort foods," like the ever-popular lasagna; baked macaroni with Vermont cheese; and walnut sauce with spaghetti.

And if you are a pumpkin pie aficionado, wait until you try the creamy pumpkin sauce with bow ties.

And my half-dressed pasta dish makes you realize how easy and how much fun cooking can be—with loads of great taste!

Spaghetti with Fresh Basil

"Simple and alluring" is what this dish says to me.

1 pound spaghetti
1 cup toasted bread crumbs
½ cup extra-virgin olive oil
1 tablespoon unsalted butter
3 cloves garlic
1 cup fresh basil, coarsely chopped
½ cup fresh Italian parsley, chopped
½ cup grated Parmesan cheese
1 tablespoon orange zest, minced
¼ teaspoon crushed red pepper (optional)
Salt to taste (optional)
Freshly ground black pepper to taste

SERVES 4 TO 6

Cook the pasta (see page xiii).

Brown the bread crumbs in a medium skillet. Remove them and set aside.

Add the oil and butter to the skillet and brown the garlic, add the basil and parsley. Drain the pasta and toss in a serving bowl with the oil mixture. Add the bread crumbs, cheese, orange zest, red pepper, salt, and pepper. Toss well and serve.

❧ Fettuccine with New York Apples

New York State is the largest apple-producing state, which is news to a lot of people. And although there are countless restaurants in New York that have pasta on their menus, none serves it with apples, so this is an original.

1 pound fettuccine
Juice of 1 lemon
5 sweet apples, peeled and sliced
4 tablespoons unsalted butter
½ tablespoon ground cinnamon
½ cup golden raisins
1 tablespoon pumpkin pie spice
8 ounces low-fat sharp cheddar cheese, shredded

SERVES 4 TO 6

Preheat the oven to 350°F. Grease a 12- × 7-inch rectangular baking dish.

Cook the pasta (see page xiii). Drain the pasta and return to the pot.

Add the lemon juice to the apple slices. Then add the butter, cinnamon, raisins, and pumpkin pie spice, and toss together to combine.

Layer half the pasta, half the apples, and half the cheese. Repeat the procedure to use up the remaining ingredients. Cover the dish with foil and bake at 350°F for 30 minutes. Remove the foil and bake an additional 10 minutes. Serve hot.

Pasta Crêpes (meatless)

8 large manicotti (tubes)
1 pound ricotta (low-fat or nonfat)
½ cup grated Parmesan cheese, plus extra for serving
2 tablespoons chopped Italian parsley
¼ teaspoon ground nutmeg
1 teaspoon dried basil
Freshly ground black pepper to taste
Salt to taste (optional)
1 quart marinara sauce (page 178)

SERVES 4 TO 6

Preheat the oven to 350°F. Grease a baking dish.

Cook the pasta (see page xiii). Drain, rinse in cold water, and drain well again.

Meanwhile, in a large bowl, combine the ricotta, Parmesan cheese, parsley, nutmeg, basil, pepper, and salt and mix well.

Spoon some of the marinara sauce into the bottom of the baking dish. Fill the manicotti with the cheese mixture, then ladle the remaining sauce on top of each tube. Bake at 350°F, uncovered, for 20 minutes, or until it begins to bubble. Sprinkle grated cheese on top and serve.

Stuffed Shells (Meatless): Substitute two packages of large stuffing shells for the manicotti. Any remaining filling may be frozen for future use.

Pasta with Walnut Sauce

I like to serve walnut sauce with pasta as an appetizer before roast turkey, duck, or goose.

1 pound spaghetti
1 large onion, minced
1 tablespoon extra-virgin olive oil
3 tablespoons unsalted butter
2 tablespoons all-purpose flour
1 cup beef stock
1 cup whole milk
¼ pound shelled walnuts
1½ cups half-and-half
¼ teaspoon white pepper
¼ teaspoon freshly ground nutmeg
Salt to taste (optional)

SERVES 4 TO 6

Cook the pasta (see page xiii).

In a medium skillet, sauté the onion in the olive oil until translucent. Add the butter and flour and stir until it turns golden brown. Whisk in the beef stock, add the milk, and cook for 8 minutes.

Meanwhile, purée the walnuts with the half-and-half in a food processor or blender, and add to the skillet with the pepper, nutmeg, and salt. Stir and reduce over high heat for 10 minutes. Toss the pasta and sauce together and serve.

Pasta with Chopped Egg

This simple dish is extremely tasty and satisfying.

¾ pound angel hair
2 tablespoons extra-virgin olive oil
2 tablespoons capers, chopped
1 cup chicken stock, heated
¼ teaspoon dried savory
Freshly ground black pepper to taste
Salt to taste (optional)
4 hard-boiled eggs, peeled and finely chopped
3 tablespoons low-fat or nonfat ranch dressing

SERVES 4 TO 6

Cook the pasta (see page xiii). Drain well and return to the pot. Add the olive oil, capers, stock, savory, pepper, and salt, and toss well. Add the eggs and ranch dressing. Toss again and serve immediately.

Pasta with Sour Cream

1 pound spaghetti
¼ pound mushrooms, sliced
1 tablespoon extra-virgin olive oil
1 tablespoon unsalted butter
1 tablespoon flour
2 cups nonfat sour cream
1 dozen green olives, chopped
½ teaspoon ground turmeric
¼ teaspoon white pepper
Salt to taste (optional)
½ cup pasta water
¼ cup chopped Italian parsley

SERVES 4 TO 6

Cook the pasta (see page xiii). Reserve ½ cup pasta water when draining.
In a large skillet, sauté the mushrooms in the olive oil and butter. Stir in the flour, and cook for 4 minutes. Reduce the heat to low and gently blend in the sour cream. Add the olives, turmeric, pepper, salt, and pasta water. Toss with the pasta and parsley and serve.

Noodles with Peppercorn Sauce

This dish is a great appetizer to serve prior to eating roast beef or steak.

¾ cup thinly sliced shallots
½ cup unsalted butter
3 cups beef stock
3 tablespoons crushed peppercorns
¾ cup brandy
2 cups heavy cream
¼ teaspoon ground mustard
Salt to taste (optional)
1 pound noodles
½ cup chopped Italian parsley

SERVES 4 TO 6

In a large skillet, sauté the shallots in butter until the shallots are translucent. Pour in the beef stock and add the peppercorns. Over high heat, reduce the sauce by half, stirring occasionally, for about 15 minutes.

Add the brandy, cream, mustard, and salt, and again reduce by half, stirring occasionally, about 20 minutes.

Cook the pasta (see page xiii). In a large bowl, combine the cooked pasta, sauce, and parsley. Toss well and serve.

❧ Pasta with Asparagus and Marsala for the First Day of Spring

Italian Marsala is a dessert wine that adds a distinct full flavor to pasta. And it seems to be springtime when the asparagus begins to appear in my greengrocer's.

8 ounces fresh asparagus, peeled and cut into 2-inch pieces
4 ounces fresh mushrooms, sliced
2 tablespoons unsalted butter
¾ cup plus 1 tablespoon Marsala wine
1½ cups beef stock
Freshly ground black pepper to taste
Salt to taste (optional)
1 pound ziti or penne
Parsley sprigs for garnish

SERVES 4 TO 6

❧

In a large skillet, sauté the asparagus and mushrooms in the butter and add 1 tablespoon of Marsala wine. Remove the vegetables when tender and set aside. Add to the skillet the remaining wine, beef stock, pepper, and salt and simmer for 25 to 30 minutes.

Meanwhile, cook the pasta (see page xiii).

When the sauce has thickened, add the cooked pasta to the skillet with the asparagus and mushrooms. Simmer for an additional 5 minutes, garnish with parsley, and serve.

Noodle Pudding

12 ounces wide noodles
2 egg yolks
3 tablespoons unsalted butter, melted
¾ cup brown sugar
1 cup golden raisins
Freshly grated nutmeg
1 tablespoon pumpkin pie spice
⅛ teaspoon salt
¼ cup sliced almonds
3 egg whites

SERVE 6 TO 8

Preheat the oven to 350°F. Grease a 13- × 9- × 2-inch baking dish.
Cook the pasta (see page xiii). Rinse, drain well, and cool.

In a large bowl, add the egg yolks and beat. Add the pasta, butter, brown sugar, raisins, nutmeg, pumpkin pie spice, salt, and almonds.

Separately beat the egg whites until stiff and fold into the mixture in the large bowl; pour the mixture into the baking dish. Bake at 350°F, covered, for 50 to 60 minutes. Serve.

Spinach Fettuccine Omelette

8 ounces spinach fettuccine, broken in half

6 large eggs

6 tablespoons whole milk

Freshly ground black pepper to taste

Pinch salt (optional)

3 tablespoons unsalted butter

¼ pound cooked ham, ¼ inch thick, cut into strips, ¼ inch wide,
   3 inches long

2 tablespoons Dijon mustard

1 cup sliced mushrooms, lightly sautéed in ½ tablespoon butter

EACH OMELETTE SERVES 2

Cook the pasta (see page xiii).

In a large mixing bowl, combine the eggs with the milk, pepper, and salt and beat lightly. In an omelette pan, melt 1½ tablespoons butter. Pour half the eggs into the pan. Layer the cooked pasta strands across the mixture down the center. Sprinkle with half the ham. As the eggs set on the outer edges of the pan, use a fork and draw them toward the center of the pan. Repeat and shake the pan to allow the uncooked eggs to set and cook. Repeat until the egg almost forms a large pancake. Spoon the mustard into the center of the omelette, and spread half the mushrooms on top. With a spatula, lift up and fold over the mushrooms. When the omelette sets, slide it onto a serving dish; fold a second time, if desired. Repeat the procedure for a second omelette.

Pasta with Danish Blue Cheese

Danish blue cheese makes this all happen.

1 pound wagon wheels
2½ cups low-fat milk
2 tablespoons all-purpose flour
¼ teaspoon ground mustard
⅛ teaspoon ground turmeric
Freshly ground black pepper to taste
8 ounces Danish blue cheese, crumbled
Salt to taste (optional)

SERVES 4 TO 6

Cook the pasta (see page xiii).

Meanwhile, in a medium saucepan heat the milk, and stir in the flour, mustard, turmeric, and pepper over low heat. Then add the cheese and continue to stir. Add the salt to taste. Cook until thickened and spoon over the pasta. Serve.

Variation: Substitute Oregon blue cheese.

Lasagna

Lasagna would be my pasta of choice whenever Mom asked what I'd like her to make special for me. She puts so much love (and ingredients) into it that it becomes a main course!

1 pound lasagna
1 pound low-fat ricotta cheese
1 large egg, beaten
2 egg whites, beaten
½ cup grated Parmesan cheese
½ cup chopped Italian parsley
¼ teaspoon ground nutmeg
¼ teaspoon dried basil
Freshly ground black pepper to taste
Salt to taste (optional)
1 quart tomato meat sauce
8 ounces mozzarella cheese, shredded
1 pound Italian sausages, cooked and sliced (optional)

SERVES 6 TO 8 AS A MAIN COURSE

Cook the pasta (see page xiii). (If using uncooked noodles, follow manufacturer's directions.) Drain, rinse in cold water, and drain again.

Preheat the oven to 350°F. Grease a 13- × 9- × 2-inch baking dish.

In a large mixing bowl, mix together the ricotta, eggs, Parmesan cheese, parsley, nutmeg, basil, pepper, and salt. Spoon some of the sauce into the baking dish. Make a layer of pasta on the bottom, spread some ricotta mixture on top, and sprinkle with mozzarella. Layer the sausages if using. Ladle on some of the sauce. Repeat the procedure until all the ingredients except the sauce are used up. End with pasta on top with a coating of sauce; reserve some sauce to serve with the pasta. Cover and bake at 350°F for about 40 minutes. Let stand before serving, and serve with extra sauce.

Mexican Lasagna

Double this recipe and you have a great party dish for any season anywhere!

1 pound lasagna
Two 15-ounce cans refried beans
2 cloves garlic, minced
½ teaspoon chili seasoning
½ teaspoon dried oregano
½ cup chopped fresh cilantro
Salt to taste (optional)
Freshly ground black pepper to taste
2 cups shredded Monterey Jack Cheese
2 cups tomato sauce
1 cup sour cream
One 2- to 3-ounce can sliced olives, drained

SERVES 6 TO 8 AS A MAIN COURSE

Cook the pasta in boiling water until *al dente*. Drain, rinse in cold water, and drain again.

Preheat the oven to 350°F. Grease a 13- × 9- × 2-inch baking dish.

In a large mixing bowl, mix together the beans, garlic, chili, oregano, cilantro, salt, and pepper. Spoon some sauce into the baking dish. Make a layer of pasta on the bottom, spread some bean mixture on top, and sprinkle with cheese. Ladle on some of the sauce. Repeat the process until all the ingredients except the sauce are used up, ending with pasta on top with a coating of sauce. Cover and bake at 350°F for about 25 minutes. Remove and cover with sour cream, top with olives, and let stand for 5 minutes. Serve.

Spinach Lasagna

1 pound lasagna
1 pound ricotta cheese
One 10-ounce package chopped frozen spinach, thawed
1 large egg, beaten
2 egg whites, beaten
½ cup grated Parmesan cheese
½ cup chopped Italian parsley
¼ teaspoon ground nutmeg
¼ teaspoon dried basil
Freshly ground black pepper to taste
Salt to taste (optional)
4 cups tomato meat sauce
8 ounces low-fat mozzarella cheese, shredded

SERVES 6 TO 8 AS A MAIN COURSE

Cook the pasta in boiling water until al dente. Drain, rinse in cold water, and drain again.

Preheat the oven to 350°F. Grease a 13- × 9- × 2-inch baking dish.

In a large mixing bowl, mix together the ricotta, spinach, eggs, Parmesan cheese, parsley, nutmeg, basil, pepper, and salt. Spoon some sauce into the baking dish. Make a layer of pasta on the bottom, spread some ricotta mixture on top, and sprinkle with mozzarella. Ladle on some of the sauce. Repeat the process until all the ingredients except the sauce are used up, ending with pasta on top with a coating of sauce; reserve some sauce to serve with the pasta. Cover and bake at 350°F for about 40 minutes and let stand before serving. Serve with extra sauce.

❧ Pumpkin Tortellini for Halloween

These specialty pastas are available with various fillings, but I thought this would be perfect for a night of ghouls and goblins!!

1 pound pumpkin-filled tortellini
½ cup unsalted butter
½ cup light cream
⅛ teaspoon dried dill
⅛ teaspoon ground nutmeg
¼ teaspoon ground white pepper
⅛ teaspoon ground turmeric
½ cup grated Parmesan cheese

SERVES 4 TO 6

❧

Cook the pasta (see page xiii).

Meanwhile, in a medium skillet, melt the butter over low heat. Add in the cream, dill, nutmeg, pepper, turmeric, and Parmesan cheese. Stir constantly for about 5 minutes. Drain the pasta and toss with the sauce.

Bow Ties with Pumpkin Sauce

I serve this dish in the autumn and everyone raves about it. Of course, canned pumpkin is available all year round and you can enjoy it at any time.

6 shallots, peeled and chopped
2 tablespoons unsalted butter
½ cup chicken stock
1½ cups canned pumpkin purée
1 cup light cream
4 tablespoons grated Parmesan cheese, plus extra for sprinkling each
  dish
¼ teaspoon ground nutmeg
½ teaspoon ground mustard
Freshly ground black pepper to taste
Salt to taste (optional)
1 pound bow tie pasta

SERVES 4 TO 6

In a large saucepan, cook the shallots in the butter until soft. Add the stock and simmer.

Stir in the pumpkin, cream, and grated Parmesan. Reduce the heat to simmer, and add the nutmeg, mustard, pepper, and salt. Cover, and continue to cook over low heat for about 25 minutes.

Meanwhile, cook the pasta (see page xiii). Toss the pasta with sauce and serve.

Pasta with French Gruyère Cheese

The nutty flavor of Gruyère cheese is a big favorite with French cooks, with good reason.

1 pound noodles
6 tablespoons unsalted butter
6 tablespoons grated Gruyère cheese
Freshly ground black pepper to taste
Salt to taste (optional)

SERVES 4 TO 6

Cook the pasta (see page xiii). Drain and immediately toss with butter, cheese, pepper, and salt. Serve.

Moroccan Couscous

Moroccan couscous is steamed and is an excellent accompaniment to everyday entrées, but here I have presented it more as a pilaf and it can easily be adapted to serving with meat, fish, and chicken. It also makes a great stew.

1 ½ cups couscous
3 cups chicken stock
1 teaspoon extra-virgin olive oil
½ teaspoon ground turmeric
½ teaspoon ground cumin
½ cup golden raisins
Salt to taste (optional)

SERVES 4 TO 6

In a medium saucepan, combine the couscous, chicken stock, olive oil, turmeric, cumin, and raisins and bring to a boil.

The couscous will absorb the liquid in about 10 minutes. Add the salt and serve.

Rigatoni with Herb Toast

Croutons added to salads are a favorite. Here, I've created an herb toast that marries with the pasta.

¾ cup extra-virgin oil
¼ teaspoon dried oregano
8 slices white bread with crusts, ends trimmed
½ pound rigatoni
4 cloves garlic
⅛ teaspoon dried thyme
½ cup chopped Italian parsley
Juice of ½ lemon
Freshly ground black pepper to taste
Salt to taste (optional)
¼ cup grated Parmesan cheese

SERVES 4

Preheat the broiler.

In a small bowl, mix ¼ cup olive oil with the oregano. Place the bread on cookie sheets and brush with the olive oil and oregano mixture. Place under the broiler and toast lightly; turn over, brush with more mixture, and toast. Cut into 1-inch squares.

Meanwhile, cook the pasta (see page xiii). In a medium skillet, heat the remaining olive oil, brown the garlic until it turns golden, and discard it.

Drain the pasta and immediately toss it with the remaining oil. Add the thyme, parsley, lemon juice, pepper, and salt. Add the herb toast and cheese, toss together, and serve.

Half-Dressed Pasta

Here is the quintessential recipe for those of us who love lightly dressed pasta in every way.

1 pound spaghetti
1 cup toasted bread crumbs
½ cup extra-virgin olive oil
3 cloves garlic
1 teaspoon dried thyme
Freshly ground black pepper to taste
Salt to taste (optional)
¼ teaspoon crushed red pepper (optional)

SERVES 4 TO 6

Cook the pasta (see page xiii).

Toast the bread crumbs in a medium skillet. Remove when lightly browned and set aside.

In a medium skillet, heat the oil and sauté the garlic until it turns golden and discard it.

Drain the pasta and immediately toss with the oil, thyme, pepper, salt, crushed red pepper, and the toasted bread crumbs. Serve.

Chop one 2-ounce can of drained anchovy fillet. Add to hot oil and do not cook any further.

⤙ Pasta with Marinara Sauce

Again, simplicity is the key word here—and taste!

1 small onion, chopped
2 cloves garlic
¼ cup extra-virgin olive oil
One 35-ounce can Italian plum tomatoes, undrained and coarsely
    chopped
1 teaspoon salt
2 pinches dried basil
1 pinch dried thyme
Freshly ground black pepper to taste
3 ounces tomato paste (optional)
3 ounces water (optional)
1 pound pasta of your choice

SERVES 4 TO 5

In a large skillet, sauté the onion and garlic in the olive oil for about 5 minutes. And the tomatoes, with their juices, to the skillet. Add the salt, basil, thyme, and pepper. Cook, covered, for about 10 minutes; stir and cook, uncovered, for another 20 to 25 minutes.

If you like a thicker sauce, add the tomato paste and water with the tomatoes. While the sauce is simmering, cook the pasta (see page xiii). When ready, serve the sauce over the pasta.

Spaghetti with Szechuan Peanut Sauce

The local Chinese takeout kept sending me their signature peanut sauce, but I decided to make my own version. I sent this dish for their approval and the chef asked for my recipe.

2 tablespoons peanut oil
2 tablespoons sesame oil
½ cup scallions, thinly sliced
2 tablespoons rice vinegar
2 tablespoons sugar
4 tablespoons dark soy sauce
1 pound spaghetti
1¼ cups chunky peanut butter
2 tablespoons chili paste
2 cups chicken stock
2 tablespoons toasted sesame seeds

SERVES 4 TO 6

In a medium saucepan, heat the peanut oil and sesame oil and sauté the scallions until translucent. Add the vinegar, sugar, and soy sauce. Blend thoroughly.

Meanwhile, cook the pasta (see page xiii).

Add the peanut butter and chili paste to the saucepan, blend, and add the chicken stock. Mix well. Reduce slightly over high heat for about 5 minutes. Toss with the spaghetti, sprinkle on sesame seeds, and serve.

Baked Macaroni and Cheese

On an episode of Live with Regis & Kathie Lee, I made this dish—the all-American perennial favorite—during the 1996 Summer Olympics.

12 ounces elbow macaroni
2 tablespoons all-purpose flour
Salt to taste (optional)
¼ teaspoon ground mustard
⅛ teaspoon ground turmeric
Freshly ground black pepper to taste (optional)
2½ cups low-fat milk
8 ounces or more grated cheddar cheese
¼ cup grated onion (optional)
⅓ cup unflavored bread crumbs

SERVE 4 TO 6

❧

Preheat the oven to 350°F.

Cook the pasta (see page xiii). Meanwhile, in a medium saucepan, combine the flour, salt, and spices. Stir in the milk and mix well. Add half the cheese and onion and stir until melted.

In a buttered casserole dish, add the pasta.

Pour the cheese mixture over the pasta. Sprinkle any remaining cheese evenly over the top, and then sprinkle the bread crumbs over all. Place in the oven and bake for 30 minutes, or until bubbly and brown on top.

Georgia Pasta

Everywhere you turn in Georgia there's a Peachtree Avenue—a "Peachtree" this and a "Peachtree" that. Years ago I created this recipe with Peachtree Schnapps, and if you didn't catch me making it on TV, here it is.

¾ pound fettuccine
3 medium shallots, chopped
2 tablespoons unsalted butter
1 cup heavy cream
One 4½-ounce jar peach baby food (4½ ounces or ½ cup puréed peaches)
4 ounces mushrooms, sliced
2 egg yolks
⅛ teaspoon white pepper
2½ ounces peach schnapps

SERVES 4 TO 6

Cook the pasta (see page xiii).

In a medium skillet, sauté the shallots in the butter until translucent. Add the cream, peaches, mushrooms, egg yolks, and pepper. Add the schnapps. Cook over medium heat until thickened slightly, 4 to 6 minutes. Toss with the noodles and serve.

~Taiwanese Pasta

½ *bunch fresh broccoli or one 10-ounce package frozen broccoli*
1 *pound fettuccine*
2 *tablespoons sesame seeds*
3 *tablespoons extra-virgin olive oil*
3 *cloves garlic*
1 *red bell pepper, seeded and cut into strips*
½ *cup water*
3 *tablespoons soy sauce*
½ *teaspoon ground ginger*
⅛ *teaspoon white pepper*
1 *teaspoon sugar*
Salt to taste

SERVES 4 TO 6

Trim the leaves and tough ends from each stalk of broccoli, and peel off the skin. Cut the stalks into 1-inch-long pieces and cut the head into small florets. Set aside.

Cook the pasta (see page xiii).

In a large skillet, toast the sesame seeds until golden. Set aside. Add the oil to the skillet and sauté the garlic until golden, then discard. Add the broccoli and red pepper strips to the skillet, and stir-fry for 1 minute over high heat. Mix together the water, soy sauce, ginger powder, pepper, and sugar, then add to the skillet, cover, and reduce the heat to low, and cook until the broccoli is just tender but firm, about 5 minutes. Toss with the fettuccine and sesame seeds. Add the salt and serve.

⤳ Mother's Day Pasta

I am a firm believer that Mother's Day should not be an annual event but a weekly occasion. This sauce is every bit as delicate and memorable. It reminds me of a special bouquet of roses I sent to Mom. They were a light, delicate pink—not American Beauty, but an unusual variety.

1 pound penne
¼ cup unsalted butter
¼ cup all-purpose flour
2 cups low-fat milk
½ cup grated Parmesan cheese
⅛ teaspoon ground nutmeg
⅛ teaspoon white pepper
2 tablespoons tomato sauce
Salt to taste (optional)

SERVES 4 TO 6

❧

Cook the pasta (see page xiii).

In a small saucepan, melt the butter. Add the flour, whisk, and slowly add the milk and cheese. Simmer for 12 to 15 minutes, or until thickened. Remove from the heat and whisk in the nutmeg, pepper, and tomato sauce. Add the salt. In a large bowl, combine the pasta and sauce. Toss well and serve.

Fusilli with Arugula for Memorial Day

If you have never tasted arugula in a salad, you would not realize that its peppery, bitter taste is ideal for this warm-weather sauce, which I first made for a brunch in the Hamptons on Memorial Day.

1 pound fusilli
1 bunch arugula, well rinsed
¼ cup extra-virgin olive oil
1 clove garlic or more to taste
3 tablespoons unsalted butter
¼ teaspoon white pepper
½ cup grated Parmesan cheese
½ cup heavy cream

SERVES 4 TO 6

Cook the pasta (see page xiii).

Purée the arugula with the olive oil in a food processor. Add the garlic, butter, pepper, cheese, and cream. Place in a saucepan and simmer for 5 minutes, or until thickened. Toss with the pasta and serve.

Pasta for the Kids

I've included a chapter of pasta recipes designated for children. Of course, they are perfectly OK for "big kids"—moms and dads, aunts and uncles, grandmas, grandpas, nieces, nephews, and cousins.

Pasta is naturally "kid friendly" and parents should be happy that such a wholesome food is embraced by all ages. When pasta is packed for school lunch there is no swapping.

In our "Little Chefs" program at our "Cooking with Love" schools, we had six-, seven-, and eight-year-olds building lasagna, stuffing shells, and actually making pasta dough.

I remember children who never washed greens, such as fresh spinach, would enjoy it raw or steamed because they helped to wash and prepare it.

Children are great copycats and will try things their older brothers and sisters are eating. Ironically, presentation and eye appeal are "extra important to growing tastes." Good eating habits and patterns learned and practiced during the growing years form the basis of lifelong food habits, because children are born without food prejudices.

And many a day a dish of pastina with a little butter is kids' comfort food (although I'd prefer a little olive oil). And for kids these favorite recipes are sweet, fun, and nutritionally a low-fat energizer. They are fast, easy, and a non-cook can do it.

Jolly Giant Pasta

8 ounces ditalini
2 tablespoons unsalted butter
One 15-ounce can corn kernels, drained
½ cup chicken or beef stock
¼ cup grated Parmesan cheese
Salt to taste (optional)

SERVES 4

Cook the pasta (see page xiii).

Meanwhile, in a medium saucepan, add the butter, corn, and chicken stock. Stir in the cooked pasta. Add the Parmesan cheese and salt.

Ditalini with Peas: For the corn, substitute one 10-ounce package of frozen peas and cook as directed above.

❧ Peanut Butter Pasta

This sweet, nutty pasta is a special treat. Serve with slices of crisp, fresh apples and peas and orange sections.

¼ *pound pasta rings, cooked and cooled*
8 *ounces ricotta cheese*
½ *cup dark raisins*
¼ *cup sliced almonds*
½ *cup grape jelly*
2 *tablespoons water*
½ *cup creamy peanut butter*

SERVES 4 TO 6

Mix the cooked pasta with the ricotta cheese, raisins, and almonds. In a small saucepan, add the jelly and water, stir in the peanut butter, and heat until warm. Drizzle heated peanut butter sauce over top of individual pasta servings.

Wagon **T**rain

This pasta is so simple that the kids can help measure the milk and cheese.

½ pound wagon wheel pasta
1½ cups whole milk
8 ounces cheddar cheese, grated (more if desired)
6 to 8 nonfat beef franks, sliced

SERVES 4 TO 6

Cook the pasta (see page xiii).

In a large saucepan, heat the milk and cheese, and add the franks. Pour the sauce over the pasta and serve.

Alphabet Pasta

1 quart chicken stock
8 ounces alphabet pasta
2 large egg whites
2 tablespoons grated Parmesan cheese

SERVES 4 TO 6

In a medium saucepan, bring the stock to a boil and add the pasta. When the pasta is almost done, add the egg whites and quickly stir. Add the cheese and serve.

Oh! Baloney

Every American mom has baloney in the fridge. Here's a great last-minute lunch.

½ *pound pasta rings*
1 *cup whole milk*
8 *ounces American cheese, shredded*
¼ *pound baloney, cut into strips*

SERVES 4

Cook the pasta (see page xiii).
Heat the milk and cheese and add the baloney. Serve over the pasta.

Mini Raviolis

Frozen raviolis are often a wonderful convenience—but there is no reason to buy that expensive dairy-case sauce to go with them when you can make your own fresh. (See page 157 for basic sauces.)

1 pound frozen mini raviolis, cheese- or meat-filled
2 cups of your favorite pasta sauce
Grated Parmesan cheese

SERVES 4 TO 6

Cook the pasta (see page xiii).

In a small saucepan heat the sauce. Top each serving of pasta with the sauce and garnish with the cheese.

Pasta with Butter

Every little guy and big guy loves pasta with just plain old butter. Pasta in the form of alphabets, little stars (stellini), pastina, and acini di pepe are all great candidates.

This was my lunch many a time when I was young and cholesterol wasn't a worry. Of course, now I would dress it up with garlic, parsley, or hot pepper.

8 ounces stellini, alphabets, or your favorite pasta
3 tablespoons unsalted butter
Grated Parmesan cheese

SERVES 2 TO 4

Cook the pasta (see page xiii). Toss with butter and cheese and serve.

Pasta with Ketchup

So you think The Love Chef has gone mad? Every once in a while both little and "big" kids yearn for the tangy sweet combo of commercial ketchup, meat, and cheese! Chow down on them!

8 ounces spaghetti rings
4 ounces ground beef or turkey
Cheese of choice, grated
4 ounces ketchup

SERVES 2 TO 4

Cook the pasta (see page xiii).

Cook the ground meat in a nonstick pan until no longer pink, and combine the cooked beef with the pasta and cheese. Add the ketchup and serve.

Cookie Cutters

6 lasagna noodles (not the curly kind)
1 teaspoon extra-virgin olive oil
One 13- to 14-ounce can low-sodium chicken broth
2 tablespoons grated Parmesan cheese

SERVES 2 TO 4

Cook the pasta (see page xiii). Add the olive oil to the water.

Using a favorite cookie cutter, cut out shapes from the cooked lasagna. In a small saucepan, heat the broth and add the cutouts. Serve the pasta cutouts with some broth and garnish with cheese.

Black and White Ice Cream Pasta

8 jumbo shells
1 tablespoon vanilla extract
1 teaspoon ground cinnamon
¼ teaspoon ground nutmeg
½ pint vanilla ice cream or frozen vanilla yogurt
1 cup chocolate sauce or syrup

SERVES 4

Cook the pasta, but use half the recommended amount of water (see page xiii), bring to a boil, then add the vanilla, cinnamon, and nutmeg to the water.

When the pasta is cooked, drain (do not rinse), and freeze quickly to cool down. When the pasta is cool, fill the shells with ice cream, and pour chocolate sauce over the shells.

Pasta and Lima Beans

½ pound wagon wheel pasta
2 tablespoons unsalted butter
One 15-ounce can large lima (butter) beans, drained
1 cup chicken stock
¼ cup grated Parmesan cheese
Salt to taste (optional)

SERVES 4

Cook the pasta (see page xiii).

Meanwhile, in a medium saucepan combine the butter, beans, and chicken stock, and mix in the cooked pasta, Parmesan cheese, and salt. Serve.

Glossary

Amaretto liqueur: An almond-flavored liqueur.

Balsamic vinegar (aceto balsamico): A slightly acidic, somewhat sweet vinegar made from pressed grapes and then aged in wood. It has a distinctive dark amber color.

Basil: An aromatic herb, available fresh or dried, that has a sweet but pungent flavor. It is a key herb in the Italian kitchen.

Bread crumbs: Store-bought dry bread crumbs are sold plain or flavored, but fresh bread crumbs can easily be made at home with hardened Italian bread.

Caciocavallo: A table and grating cheese that is mild when young and sharpens as it ages. It is also available studded with whole peppercorns, making it a pungent companion for cured meats and assorted *antipasti*.

Cannellini: Large white Italian kidney beans, available in both dried and canned forms.

Chicken cutlets: White meat flattened for quick sautéing.

Crushed red pepper: Dried chili peppers that are crushed into flakes. In addition to their use in recipes, crushed red pepper makes a table condiment that gives zing to sauces, vegetables, and soups.

Fennel seeds: An anise-flavored spice similar to the fresh vegetable fennel.

Garlic bulb/clove: A whole head or bulb of garlic is composed of several individual cloves, which break away easily for cooking purposes.

Italian parsley: Characterized by flat leaves in contrast to its curly counterpart. This parsley's less-acidic taste is best suited for Italian recipes.

Italian sausage: Traditionally, a pork sausage, available in sweet or hot varieties, made with distinctive spices, especially fennel seeds, which give it an anise flavor.

Marsala: A dessert wine from Sicily with the rich, distinctive taste of burnt sugar. It is available dry and sweet.

Mascarpone: A sweet, rich, and creamy cheese made from cow's milk.

Olive oil: Italian olive oils are the pure products of the olive tree and have been filtered to remove sediment. For the past 8,000 years, man has been utilizing this amazing tree and its fruits.

> **Extra-light:** Very mild-tasting and light in color; great for frying and ideal for baking; has the same calories as the regular.

> **Extra-virgin:** Made from the first cold pressing of the olives, with less than one percent acidity. Very fragrant, full-bodied, and greener in color than most other olive oils. Use it where oil is prominent, as in salads, dips, and sauces.

> **Pure:** A refined blend of olive oils having a less fruity taste. Use whenever the recipe calls for oil in general cooking.

> **Virgin:** Still from the first pressing but most probably heat is involved to create the pressure. This oil has a higher acidity, and is a fragrant addition to recipes using fish and in marinades.

Pancetta: Italian bacon that is cured with salt and spices.

Parmesan cheese (Parmigiano-Reggiano): A very hard and dry cheese made with skimmed cow's milk, mild but rich in flavor. It is used principally for grating, but is also great for nibbling. Usually imported from Italy, Parmesan cheese is also made domestically.

Pine nuts (pignoli): These come from pine trees and look like tiny white beans. They have a sweet and flavorful taste.

Polenta: A mush made from cornmeal.

Prosciutto: A salted, air-cured ham, usually sliced very thin and eaten raw or sautéed as an ingredient in a recipe. The Italian variety is preferred, although prosciutto is also produced in the United States.

Ricotta cheese: A cheese that is as creamy as cottage cheese and is made mainly from cow's milk. It is also available in low-fat and nonfat varieties. It has a slightly sweet flavor.

Romano cheese: A hard cheese made with sheep's milk mostly used for grating. It is sharper in flavor than Parmesan. Although the bulk is imported from Italy, Romano is also manufactured domestically.

Tomatoes, canned plum: Marzano, Italy, is known for its plum tomatoes, many of which are canned and exported. Of course, California is also a major packer of tomatoes. Usually plum tomatoes are canned with juice, or some are canned in a heavier purée. Experiment with brands of your choosing.

    Canned whole and peeled: Uncooked whole tomatoes are packed in tomato purée or tomato juice.

    Crushed: Whole, peeled, uncooked tomatoes that are crushed.

Tomato paste: Made from tomatoes that were cooked for several hours, strained, and reduced to a thick concentrate.

Tomato purée: Tomatoes that are cooked briefly and strained to make a purée, with a fairly thick consistency.

Tomato sauce: Cooked tomatoes with the addition of seasonings and sometimes tomato paste.

Things to Know

3 teaspoons	1 tablespoon
2 tablespoons	1 ounce
4 tablespoons	¼ cup
16 tablespoons	1 cup
2 cups	1 pint
4 cups	1 quart
1 pound granulated sugar	2 cups
1 pound confectioners' sugar	2⅓ cups
¼ pound butter or 1 stick	½ cup
1 pound all-purpose flour	4 cups sifted flour

Index

Hawaiian pasta with
   pineapple and shrimp,
   144
hazelnuts, pasta with
   mushrooms and, 17
hearty Irish pasta with lamb,
   76
herb toast, rigatoni with, 176
hot and spicy Puerto Rican
   pasta, 33
Hungarian noodles, 3

I

ice cream pasta, black and
   white, 196
Idaho potatoes, pasta with,
   39
Illinois pasta with steak, 99
Indiana pasta with corn and
   bits of bacon, 108
Indonesian satay pasta,
   100
Iowa pasta with pork and
   asparagus, 90
Irish pasta with lamb, hearty,
   76
Italian sausage, pasta with, for
   the Super Bowl, 67

J

Japanese curly noodles with
   beef teriyaki, 124
jolly giant pasta, 187

K

Kansas pasta with squash and
   corn, 38
Kentucky burgoo, pasta with,
   103–104
ketchup, pasta with,
   194
kids, pasta for the,
   185–197
kohlrabi, pasta with, 14
Korean pasta, 123

L

Labor Day, cold turkey for,
   66

lamb:
   chops, Nebraska pasta
      with, 81
   Colorado pasta with
      eggplant and, 78
   couscous with, 79
   curried, and tomato pasta,
      77
   hearty Irish pasta with, 76
   in Nevada pasta, 80
lasagna, 169
   in cookie cutters,
      195
   Mexican, 170
   spinach, 171
lemon sauce, farfalle and
   chicken in, 49
linguine:
   and anchovy oil, 25
   with chicken and fennel,
      60
   Grandpa's shrimp, scallop
      and cod with, 150–151
   with scallions and bread
      crumbs, 26
   with scallops, 154
liver, noodles with onions
   and, 110
lo mein, pork, 126
Louisiana pasta with spicy
   shrimp and sausage, 87

M

macaroni and cheese, baked,
   180
marinara sauce, pasta with,
   178
Marsala, pasta with asparagus
   and, for the first day of
   spring, 165
Maryland pasta with soft-shell
   crabs, 143
Massachusetts cold pasta salad
   with cranberries, 53
mayonnaise:
   in cold turkey for Labor
      Day, 66
   in Massachusetts cold pasta
      salad with cranberries,
      53
   in pasta with Idaho
      potatoes, 39
   in speedway cold pasta
      salad, 43

meat:
   -filled cannelloni, 119
   pasta with, 75–130
   sauce, pasta with, 97
meatballs:
   pasta with Swedish,
      112–113
   spaghetti and, 116–117
Mediterranean pasta, 2
Memorial Day, fusilli with
   arugula for, 184
Mexican lasagna, 170
Michigan pasta with turkey,
   73
Middle Eastern pasta, 4
mini raviolis, 192
Mississippi pasta with red
   beans, 111
Monterey Jack cheese, in
   Mexican lasagna,
      170
Moroccan couscous, 175
Mother's Day pasta, 183
mozzarella cheese:
   in Colorado pasta with
      lamb and eggplant, 78
   in lasagna, 169
   in pasta with Italian
      sausage for the Super
      Bowl, 67
   in spinach lasagna, 171
mushrooms:
   in Caribbean seafood
      pasta, 135
   fettuccine with duck, olives
      and, 50–51
   in Grandma's chicken
      tomato pasta, 55
   in New Hampshire pasta
      with venison, 109
   in pasta paprikash, 98
   in pasta stroganoff, 62
   pasta with hazelnuts and,
      17
   in spinach fettuccine
      omelette, 167
   in tetrazzini, 57
   white, noodles with garlic
      and, 34
mussels, pasta with, 148

N

Nebraska pasta with lamb
   chops, 81